CHINUA ACHEBE was born in 1930 in the village of Ogidi in Eastern Nigeria. After studying medicine and literature at the University of Ibadan, he went to work for the Nigerian Broadcasting Company in Lagos. *Things Fall Apart*, his first novel, was published in 1958. It has sold over 3,000,000 copies and has been translated in 30 languages. It was followed by *No Longer at Ease*, then *Arrow of God* (which won the first New Statesman Jock Campbell Prize), then *A Man of the People* (a novel dealing with post-independence Nigeria). *Anthills of the Savannah* was shortlisted for the Booker Prize in 1987.

Achebe has also written short stories and children's books, and *Beware Soul Brother*, a book of his poetry, won the Commonwealth Poetry Prize in 1972. A new collection of essays and literary criticism, *Hopes and Impediments*, was published by Heinemann in 1988.

Achebe has lectured at universities in Nigeria, Massachusetts and Connecticut, and among the many honours he has received are the award of a Fellowship of the Modern Language Association of America, and many honorary doctorates from universities in Britain, USA, Canada and Nigeria. He followed Heinrich Boll, the Nobel prizewinner, as the second recipient of the Scottish Arts Council Neil Gunn Fellowship. In 1987, he was recognised in Nigeria with the Nigerian National Merit Award – the country's highest award for intellectual achievement.

C. L. Innes has taught English and Comparative Literature at universities in Australia, the United States and England, where she currently lectures at the University of Kent. She has published a number of articles on African, Australian and Irish literature. Innes' most recent books are *The Devil's Own Mirror*, a comparative study on Irish and African Literature (Three Continents Press, Washington D.C.) and *Chinua Achebe* (Cambridge University Press).

Chinua Achebe and C. L. Innes are the editors of *African Short Stories* which is also available from Heinemann in the African Writers Series.

D1008364

THE HEINEMANN BOOK OF
CONTEMPORARY AFRICAN SHORT STORIES

Edited by Chinua Achebe and C. L. Innes

HEINEMANN

Heinemann International Literature and Textbooks
a division of Heinemann Educational Books Ltd
Halley Court, Jordan Hill, Oxford OX2 8EJ

Heinemann Educational Books Inc
361 Hanover Street, Portsmouth, New Hampshire, 03801, USA

Heinemann Educational Books (Nigeria) Ltd
PMB 5205, Ibadan
Heinemann Kenya Ltd
Kijabe Street, PO Box 45314, Nairobi
Heinemann Educational Boleswa
PO Box 10103, Village Post Office, Gaborone, Botswana

LONDON   EDINBURGH   MADRID
PARIS   ATHENS   BOLOGNA   MELBOURNE
SYDNEY   AUCKLAND   SINGAPORE
TOKYO   HARARE

First published by Heinemann International Literature and
Textbooks in the African Writers Series in 1992

Series Editor: Adewale Maja-Pearce

British Library Cataloguing in Publication Data

The Heinemann book of contemporary African short stories.
I. Achebe, Chinua, 1930–   II. Innes, C. L.
823.010896 [FS]

ISBN 043590566X

Photoset by Cambridge Composing (UK) Ltd., Cambridge
Printed in Great Britain by
Cox and Wyman Ltd., Reading, Berkshire

93 94 10 9 8 7 6 5 4 3 2

Contents

NORTHERN AFRICA

WEST AFRICA

Acknowledgements

The editors wish to thank all those who responded to their call for help in finding stories. In particular Nadine Gordimer, Essop Patel, Walter Oliphant, Abdulrazak Gurnah and Adewale Maja-Pearce contributed names, addresses, manuscripts and published collections which proved most valuable. Special acknowledgement for their thoughtful, detailed advice and many hours' reading should also be given to Ik Achebe, Nicola Horton and Helena Smith, without whose assistance this anthology would have been many more months in the making. And Marian Beale dealt efficiently with the considerable correspondence involved.

The editors and publishers would like to thank the following for their permission to use copyright material:

Okey Chigbo for 'The Housegirl'; Steve Chimombo for 'The Rubbish Dump' from *Namaluzi: Ten Stories from Malawi* (Dzuka Publishing Co 1984); Mia Couto and David Brookshaw (translator) for 'The Birds of God' from *Voices Made Night* (Heinemann 1990); Assia Djebar and Dorothy Blair (translator) for 'The Foreigner, Sister of the Foreign Woman' from *Loin de Medine* (Editions Albin Michel SA, Paris 1991); Hatier International, E. B. Dongala and Clive Wake (translator) for 'The Man' from *Jazz et Vin de Palme* (Hatier, Paris, 1982); Nadine Gordimer for 'Amnesty' (used by permission of Russell & Volkening and A P Watt Ltd); Abdulrazak Gurnah for 'Cages'; Saida Hagi-Dirie Herzi for 'Government by Magic Spell'; Kojo Laing for 'Vacancy for the Post of Jesus Christ'; Lindiwe Mabuza and Skotaville Publishers, Braamfontein, for 'Wake' from *One Never Knows* (Skotaville Publishers);

Jamal Mahjoub for 'Road Block'; Adewale Maja-Pearce and Longman Group UK Ltd for 'The Hotel' from *Loyalties*, (Longman); Daniel Mandishona for 'A Wasted Land'; Kyalo Mativo for 'On the Market Day' which was published in *African Commentary*, 1990; Tololwa Marti Mollel for 'A Night Out'; Ba'bila Mutia for 'The Miracle'; Njabulo S. Ndebele, Longman Group UK Ltd, Ravan Press (Pty) Ltd and Shelley Power Literary Agency Ltd for 'The Prophetess' from *Fools and Other Stories* (Longman); Ben Okri for 'Converging City' from *Incidents at the Shrine* (Secker and Warburg); Tijan M. Sallah for 'Weaverdom' from *Before the New Earth* (P. Lal Writers Workshop Books); Moyez G. Vassanji for 'Leaving' from *Uhuru Street* (Heinemann, 1991), (used by permission of the Canadian Publishers, McClelland & Stewart, Toronto).

The publishers have made every effort to trace copyright holders, but in some case without success. We shall be very glad to hear from anyone who has been inadvertently overlooked or incorrectly cited and make the necessary changes at the first opportunity.

Introduction

When Chinua Achebe and I compiled our first anthology, *African Short Stories*, we set out to include a sample of the best short fiction which had been produced by African writers until 1983, when the selection was being made. For this second anthology of more recent short fiction, we have concentrated on work which has been written and published since 1980.

Finding material for our first collection presented relatively few problems: there was a wealth of published material readily available in Africa, England and America. A number of major writers had published collections of stories which had been published by Heinemann in their African Writers Series. These included Sembene Ousmane, Ngũgĩ wa Thiong'o, Taban Lo Liyong, Nadine Gordimer, Alex La Guma, Dumbedza Marachera, Luis Bernardo Honwana, Tayeb Salih and Bessie Head, as well as Chinua Achebe himself. Other major publishers, such as Faber, Longman, Pan and Penguin, had produced and kept in print collections by Doris Lessing, Nadine Gordimer and Ama Ata Aidoo. Within the past twenty-five years, there had also been a number of journals which published good short fiction – *Black Orpheus*, *Transition*, *Drum* and *Okike* provided us with a wide range of material from all parts of the continent except the North. In addition, there were already a number of anthologies in existence, offering both material and models for our own anthology. Heinemann had more than a dozen such anthologies, some of which represented particular regions or interests such as Egypt, the South, or stories by African women writers. Most of the material we considered for our first anthology, therefore, already had the stamp of approval in terms of editorial choice and, often, critical reception.

Our first criteria for selection was literary merit, although we also hoped that we could represent writers of different regions, sexes and generations. As Chinua Achebe wrote in the Preface to the anthology, our 'selections went ahead with gratifying serendipity' to meet both considerations – literary merit and range of representation. And, as he went on to say, 'the subsequent grouping of the stories into broad geographical regions seemed a handy and practical arrangement. But any other format might have done just as well: we might have arranged the authors alphabetically or the stories chronologically, and so on.'

Collecting material for our second anthology has been a different matter. Many well-known African writers appear to have turned away from short fiction. In the past ten years, there seem to have been no new short stories by Aidoo, Ngũgĩ, Sembene, Mphahlele or Achebe, who were among the best practitioners of the art. Some collections by newer writers such as Ben Okri, Njabulo Ndebele, Farida Karodia and Adewale Maja-Pearce have appeared, but the number of such collections is small. In particular, the major publishers appear to have lost interest in putting out stories in translation – there are no new francophone or Arabic stories, although Heinemann has given us one collection by Mia Couto from Mozambique, translated from the Portuguese. Moreover, some of the journals which used to publish good short stories have disappeared: *Transition* ceased publication between 1976 and 1991; *Black Orpheus* no longer exists; *Okike* suffered from Nigeria's currency problems and paper shortages during the Eighties, and its appearance was somewhat haphazard. The one real exception to this apparent lack of writing and publication as far as the short story is concerned is South Africa, where *Staffrider* has continued over the past decade to appear fairly regularly and to publish poetry and prose of high quality. Publishers within South Africa, notably Ravan Press and Skotaville, have also put out a number of collections and anthologies of poetry and prose by a variety of writers.

At first sight one might have feared that the wellsprings of creativity for short fiction in Africa had begun to dry up in the past decade. Except in the South, it seemed, Africans were either not writing at all or had turned away from the short story as a genre. Time was running out, so we decided to advertise and see what happened. We placed advertisements in the British Council Newsletter, *Literature Matters*, in *Wasafiri*, in *West Africa*, and in *Staffrider*. All brought results: a small trickle of stories, generally well crafted and well written, made their way to us. But it was an advertisement in a new magazine called *African Commentary* which opened the floodgates. It seems that this magazine must have a substantial readership, mainly in Nigeria but also in Central Africa, East Africa, the United States and Canada. We were overwhelmed! Hundreds of stories poured in. Most were in manuscript, from previously unpublished writers; some had appeared in newspapers or small magazines, and others had been published in book form by local publishers or by the authors themselves. The quality, the writing skills, the topics, the uses of language, the concept of 'story-telling' all varied a great deal, although the majority contained much potential. What suddenly became obvious is that there is a great deal of writing going on in Africa, and that story-telling for readers rather than listeners, and the idea of being an author who creates and belongs to his story, have caught on in a big way. The fact that there are relatively few outlets for publishing such stories makes the phenomenon all the more surprising.

So what kinds of story are being written? Who is writing them? And has there been much change over the past thirty or forty years? The answer varies from region to region. In South Africa, for example, we continue to find what Chinua Achebe described as 'the painful, inescapable bond to racism' which marked the stories from there in our first anthology. Most of the South African stories we read developed the realist mode of their predecessors, portraying in harsh detail the lives of the black proletariat in the shanty towns and urban ghettos. There were an increasing number of stories by and about women, often left to carry alone the burden of providing for the day-to-day existence of their children. The figure of the indomitable African mother, struggling to find for her children – and often her menfolk – the bare necessities, waiting fearfully for news of a missing husband or son, recurs again and again in these stories from the South. She is presented as a figure of the almost intolerable suffering and injustice of the system, and at the same time of the superior morality and humanity, the sheer endurance, of black people as a whole in South Africa. When younger black women are portrayed, they are either domestic servants, secretaries or, occasionally, students. The figure of the woman household servant is most often used to focus the contrast between her hardworking and constrained life with the lifestyle and attitudes of the privileged white woman who spends her time in trivial social pursuits, and for whom the servant is less than human. Many stories respond to the Soweto uprisings and their influence, both in terms of the issues of control over education and its purpose, and concern with a generation of school-age children who have become revolutionaries and who have seen their fellow students murdered and tortured. Some of the most remarkable stores we read were in a collection called *One Never Knows*, an anthology by black South African women writers in exile, edited by Lindiwe Mabuza for Skotaville Publishers. The writers included Dulcie September, who as ANC representative in Paris was killed by a terrorist bomb in 1988, and Lindiwe Mabuza herself, who has been ANC representative in Stockholm and Washington. Lindiwe Mabuza's story, 'Wake', which we reprint here, is a particularly powerful evocation of events and the feelings they aroused in Soweto, presented through the voice of an eight-year-old girl whose best friend has been shot, and drawing on a variety of techniques and styles – realist description, dream, dialogue, drama, stream of consciousness, traditional and contemporary songs of children and adults, and political statement. These varying forms build to a rousing and unsentimentally optimistic ending as, during the funeral, the child Thoko envisions her dead friend Lwazi returned:

> Right there on the land of martyrs Lwazi rose from her narrow imprisonment, offering Thoko both her hands. They both looked at the lavatory. Both smiled and then joined their hands, making a bridge and before they could even finish squeezing the pests beween their thumb nails, the hundreds of coffins lightly rested on their joined hands. The marchers' song rose like bells at morning break and the bridge and reason for all moved to meet the marchers. Rising to crown the human rainbow was Naledi's banner, no longer an aloe in the desert! 'It is not wrong to fight for justice.'

This story is a powerful example of what is to be found in much of the best contemporary writing coming out of Africa. Such writing mingles a variety of genres which traditionally were kept separate: the political statement, the lecture, poetry, drama, and the short talk, and can be found not only in short but also longer fiction such as Ama Ata Aidoo's *Our Sister Killjoy*, Dumbedza Marachera's *The House of Hunger*, Achebe's *Anthills of the Savannah*, and Ngũgĩ's later novels. Almost all the stories we read for our first anthology belonged to the realist mode and their political message was implicit rather than explicit. Where the fantastic was referred to, it was usually distanced by being offered as an experience related by one of the characters, and which the reader could take or leave – as dream, as drunken delirium, as naive superstition perhaps. But in many of the newer stories the visionary and the fantastic are offered directly to the reader with no mediation. The story included here by the Ghanaian writer Kojo Laing is titled 'Vacancy for the post of Jesus Christ' and begins: 'When the small quick lorry was being lowered from the skies, it was discovered that it had golden wood, and many seedless guavas for the hungry.'

Similarly Ben Okri's fiction brings into conjunction the fantastic or phantasmagoric and the mundane. Both these writers and others from Africa may have been encouraged by the magic-realist fictions of Latin American novelists such as Gabriel García Marquez, but one might also see them returning to and reinventing the pre-colonial traditions which one can find in the work of Amos Tutuola, with their exuberant embrace of folk imagination, and fantasy intermingled with the everyday. In so doing, this younger generation of writers moves away from what some of them see as the binary focus of earlier African fiction, caught up in a dialogue with and opposition to the colonial powers, and concerned with identifying a unified, non-European national culture.

Although such a description does an injustice to the complexity of writing in the Sixties, it does help identify differences in direction and aim. For Okri and Laing, it is the hybridity and heterogeneity of contemporary post-colonial society which are of central interest, a multiplicity of cultures and influences which converge in the language, worlds and consciousness of the urban poor whom Okri mostly writes about, rather than the rural villagers or the educated élite who feature in the novels and stories of the Sixties. It is a world which is presented vividly, sharply, without explanation or gloss, for what it is: a world in which the supernatural and the secular, the market and the shrine, the technological and the traditional are equally valid and equally bizarre.

Okri and Laing represent a significant new kind of writing from Africa, but theirs is not the only kind. Many of the stories we received were thinly veiled political allegories or documentaries, such as Saida Herzi's 'factions' about Somalia. The stories of rural villagers, especially of the poorest and the women attempting to live with dignity in a disintegrating economy, are being written into literature. There is a greater diversity of writers, and with them a greater recognition of the variety of cultures within the African continent, including the communities of Indian and Arabic descent in Eastern and Southern Africa, the conflicts between Igbos, Yorubas and northern Islamic societies in Nigeria, the differences between the poor and the middle classes, and the politicians who are a class unto themselves. Especially we noticed this time the increasing number of women writers and also of men who were taking notice of and seeking to express a female perspective on such issues as marriage, childbearing and circumcision.

This anthology reveals the lively diversity of subjects, forms and styles which can be found in contemporary African short-story writing. The editors believe that it will give enjoyment to the general reader as well as students and teachers of African writing, and hope that it will encourage them to explore a literature which continues to develop and flourish.

C. L. Innes 1992

NJABULO S. NDEBELE

The prophetess

The boy knocked timidly on the door, while a big fluffy dog sniffed at his ankles. That dog made him uneasy; he was afraid of strange dogs and this fear made him anxious to go into the house as soon as possible. But there was no answer to his knock. Should he simply turn the doorknob and get in? What would the prophetess say? Would she curse him? He was not sure now which he feared more: the prophetess or the dog. If he stood longer there at the door, the dog might soon decide that he was up to some mischief after all. If he left, the dog might decide he was running away. And the prophetess! What would she say when she eventually opened the door to find no one there? She might decide someone had been fooling, and would surely send lightning after the boy. But then, leaving would also bring the boy another problem: he would have to leave without the holy water for which his sick mother had sent him to the prophetess.

There was something strangely intriguing about the prophetess and holy water. All that one was to do, the boy had so many times heard in the streets of the township, was fill a bottle with water and take it to the prophetess. She would then lay her hands on the bottle and pray. And the water would be holy. And the water would have curing powers. That's what his mother had said too.

The boy knocked again, this time with more urgency. But he had to be careful not to annoy the prophetess. It was getting darker and the dog continued to sniff at his ankles. The boy tightened his grip round the neck of the bottle he had just filled with water from the street tap on the other side of the street, just opposite the prophetess's house. He would hit the dog with this bottle. What's more, if the bottle broke he would stab the dog with the sharp glass. But what would the prophetess say? She would probably curse him. The boy knocked again, but this time he heard the faint voice of a woman.

'*Kena!*' the voice said.

The boy quickly turned the knob and pushed. The door did not yield. And the dog growled. The boy turned the knob again and pushed. This time the dog gave a sharp bark, and the boy knocked frantically. Then he heard the bolt shoot back, and saw the door open to reveal darkness. Half the door seemed to have disappeared into the dark. The boy felt fur brush past his leg as the dog scurried into the house.

'*Voetsek!*' the woman cursed suddenly.

The boy wondered whether the woman was the prophetess. But as he was wondering, the dog brushed past him again, slowly this time. In spite of himself, the boy felt a pleasant, tickling sensation and a slight warmth where the fur of the dog had touched him. The warmth did not last, but the tickling sensation lingered, going up to the back of his neck and seeming to caress it. Then he shivered and the sensation disappeared, shaken off in the brief involuntary tremor.

'Dogs stay out!' shouted the woman, adding, 'This is not at the white man's.'

The boy heard a slow shuffle of soft leather shoes receding into the dark room. The woman must be moving away from the door, the boy thought. He followed into the house.

'Close the door,' ordered the woman who was still moving somewhere in the dark. But the boy had already done so.

Although it was getting dark outside, the room was much darker and the fading day threw some of its waning light into the room through the windows. The curtains had not yet been drawn. 'Was it an effort to save candles?' the boy wondered. His mother had scolded him many times for lighting up before it was completely dark.

The boy looked instinctively towards the dull light coming in through the window. He was anxious, though, about where the woman was now, in the dark. Would she think he was afraid when she caught him looking out to the light? But the thick, dark green leaves of vine outside, lapping lazily against the window, attracted and held him like a spell. There was no comfort in that light; it merely reminded the boy of his fear, only a few minutes ago, when he walked under that dark tunnel of vine which arched over the path from the gate to the door. He had dared not touch that vine and its countless velvety, black, and juicy grapes that hung temptingly within reach, or rested lusciously on forked branches. Silhouetted against the darkening summer sky, the bunches of grapes had each looked like a cluster of small cones narrowing down to a point.

'Don't touch that vine!' was the warning almost everyone in Charterston township knew. It was said that the vine was all coated with thick, invisible glue. And that was how the prophetess caught all those who stole out in the night to steal her grapes. They would be glued there to the vine, and would be moaning for forgiveness throughout the cold night, until the morning, when the prophetess would come out of the house with the first rays of the sun, raise her arms into the sky, and say: 'Away, away, sinful man; go and sin no more!' Suddenly, the thief would be free, and would walk away feeling a great release that turned him into a new man. That vine; it was on the lips of everyone in the township every summer.

●

One day when the boy had played truant with three of his friends, and they were coming back from town by bus, some grown-ups in the bus were arguing about the prophetess's vine. The bus was so full that it was hard for anyone to move. The three truant friends having given their seats to grown-ups, pressed against each other in a line in the middle of the bus and could see most of the passengers.

'Not even a cow can tear away from that glue,' said a tall, dark man who had high cheek-bones. His balaclava was a careless heap on his head. His moustache, which had been finely rolled into two semi-circular horns, made him look fierce. And when he gesticulated with his tin lunch box, he looked fiercer still.

'My question is only one,' said a big woman whose big arms rested thickly on a bundle of washing on her lap. 'Have you ever seen a person caught there? Just answer that question.' She spoke with finality, and threw her defiant scepticism outside at the receding scene of men cycling home from work in single file. The bus moved so close to them that the boy had feared the men might get hit.

'I have heard of one silly chap that got caught!' declared a young man. He was sitting with others on the long seat at the rear of the bus. They had all along been laughing and exchanging ribald jokes. The young man had thick lips and red eyes. As he spoke he applied the final touches of saliva with his tongue to brown paper rolled up with tobacco.

'When?' asked the big woman. 'Exactly when, I say? Who was that person?'

'These things really happen!' said a general chorus of women.

'That's what I know,' endorsed the man with the balaclava, and then added, 'You see, the problem with some women is that they will not listen; they have to oppose a man. They just have to.'

'What is that man saying now?' asked another woman. 'This matter started off very well, but this road you are now taking will get us lost.'

'That's what I'm saying too,' said the big woman, adjusting her bundle of washing somewhat unnecessarily. She continued: 'A person shouldn't look this way or that, or take a corner here or there. Just face me straight: I asked a question.'

'These things really happen,' said the chorus again.

'That's it, good ladies, make your point; push very strongly,' shouted the young man at the back. 'Love is having women like you,' he added, much to the enjoyment of his friends. He was now smoking, and his rolled up cigarette looked small between his thick fingers.

'Although you have no respect,' said the big woman, 'I will let you know that this matter is no joke.'

'Of course this is not a joke!' shouted a new contributor. He spoke firmly and in English. His eyes seemed to burn with anger. He was young and immaculately dressed, his white shirt collar resting neatly on the collar of his jacket. A young nurse in a white uniform sat next to him. 'The mother there,' he continued, 'asks you very clearly whether you have ever seen a person caught by the supposed prophetess's supposed trap. Have you?'

'She didn't say that, man,' said the young man at the back, passing the roll to one of his friends. 'She only asked when this person was caught and who it was.' The boys at the back laughed. There was a lot of smoke now at the back of the bus.

'My question was,' said the big woman turning her head to glare at

the young man, 'have you ever seen a person caught there? That's all.'
Then she looked outside. She seemed angry now.

'Don't be angry, mother,' said the young man at the back. There
was more laughter. 'I was only trying to understand,' he added.

'And that's our problem,' said the immaculately dressed man,
addressing the bus. His voice was sure and strong. 'We laugh at
everything; just stopping short of seriousness. Is it any wonder that the
white man is still sitting on us? The mother there asked a very
straightforward question, but she is answered vaguely about things
happening. Then there is disrespectful laughter at the back there. The
truth is you have no proof. None of you. Have you ever seen anybody
caught by this prophetess? Never. It's all superstition. And so much
about this prophetess also. Some of us are tired of her stories.'

There was a stunned silence in the bus. Only the heavy drone of an
engine struggling with an overloaded bus could be heard. It was the
man with the balaclava who broke the silence.

'Young man,' he said, 'by the look of things you must be a clever,
educated person, but you just note one thing. The prophetess might
just be hearing all this, so don't be surprised when a bolt of lightning
strikes you on a hot sunny day. And we shall be there at your funeral,
young man, to say how you brought misfortune upon your head.'

Thus had the discussion ended. But the boy had remembered how,
every summer, bottles of all sizes filled with liquids of all kinds of
colours would dangle from vines and peach and apricot trees in many
yards in the township. No one dared steal fruit from those trees. Who
wanted to be glued in shame to a fruit tree? Strangely, though, only the
prophetess's trees had no bottles hanging from their branches.

•

The boy turned his eyes away from the window and focused into the
dark room. His eyes had adjusted slowly to the darkness, and he saw
the dark form of the woman shuffling away from him. She probably
wore those slippers that had a fluff on top. Old women seem to love
them. Then a white receding object came into focus. The woman wore
a white *doek* on her head. The boy's eyes followed the *doek*. It took a
right-angled turn – probably round the table. And then the dark form

of the table came into focus. The *doek* stopped, and the boy heard the screech of a chair being pulled; and the *doek* descended somewhat and was still. There was silence in the room. The boy wondered what to do. Should he grope for a chair? Or should he squat on the floor respectfully? Should he greet or wait to be greeted? One never knew with the prophetess. Why did his mother have to send him to this place? The fascinating stories about the prophetess, to which the boy would add graphic details as if he had also met her, were one thing; but being in her actual presence was another. The boy then became conscious of the smell of camphor. His mother always used camphor whenever she complained of pains in her joints. Was the prophetess ill then? Did she pray for her own water? Suddenly, the boy felt at ease, as if the discovery that a prophetess could also feel pain somehow made her explainable.

'*Lumela 'me*,' he greeted. Then he cleared his throat.

'*Eea ngoanaka*,' she responded. After a little while she asked: 'Is there something you want, little man?' It was a very thin voice. It would have been completely detached had it not been for a hint of tiredness in it. She breathed somewhat heavily. Then she coughed, cleared her throat, and coughed again. A mixture of rough discordant sounds filled the dark room as if everything was coming out of her insides, for she seemed to breathe out her cough from deep within her. And the boy wondered: if she coughed too long, what would happen? Would something come out? A lung? The boy saw the form of the woman clearly now: she had bent forward somewhat. Did anything come out of her on to the floor? The cough subsided. The woman sat up and her hands fumbled with something around her breasts. A white cloth emerged. She leaned forward again, cupped her hands and spat into the cloth. Then she stood up and shuffled away into further darkness away from the boy. A door creaked, and the white *doek* disappeared. The boy wondered what to do because the prophetess had disappeared before he could say what he had come for. He waited.

More objects came into focus. Three white spots on the table emerged. They were placed diagonally across the table. Table mats. There was a small round black patch on the middle one. Because the prophetess was not in the room, the boy was bold enough to move near the table and touch the mats. They were crocheted mats. The boy remembered the huge lacing that his mother had crocheted for the church altar. ALL SAINTS CHURCH was crocheted all over the lacing. There were a number of designs of chalices that carried the Blood of Our Lord.

Then the boy heard the sound of a match being struck. There were many attempts before the match finally caught fire. Soon, the dull, orange light of a candle came into the living room where the boy was, through a half closed door. More light flushed the living room as the woman came in carrying a candle. She looked round as if she was wondering where to put the candle. Then she saw the ashtray on the middle mat, pulled it towards her, sat down and turned the candle over into the ashtray. Hot wax dropped on to the ashtray. Then the prophetess turned the candle upright and pressed its bottom on to the wax. The candle held.

The prophetess now peered through the light of the candle at the boy. Her thick lips protruded, pulling the wrinkled skin and caving in the cheeks to form a kind of lip circle. She seemed always ready to kiss. There was a line tattooed from the forehead to the ridge of a nose that separated small eyes that were half closed by large, drooping eyelids. The white *doek* on her head was so huge that it made her face look small. She wore a green dress and a starched green cape that had many white crosses embroidered on it. Behind her, leaning against the wall, was a long bamboo cross.

The prophetess stood up again, and shuffled towards the window which was behind the boy. She closed the curtains and walked back to her chair. The boy saw another big cross embroidered on the back of her cape. Before she sat down she picked up the bamboo cross and held it in front of her.

'What did you say you wanted, little man?' she asked slowly.

'My mother sent me to ask for water,' said the boy putting the bottle of water on the table.

'To ask for water?' she asked with mild exclamation, looking up at the bamboo cross. 'That is very strange. You came all the way from home to ask for water?'

'I mean,' said the boy, 'holy water.'

'Ahh!' exclaimed the prophetess. 'You did not say what you meant, little man.' She coughed, just once. 'Sit down, little man,' she said, and continued. 'You see, you should learn to say what you mean. Words, little man, are a gift from the Almighty, the Eternal Wisdom. He gave us all a little pinch of his mind and called on us to think. That is why it is folly to misuse words or not to know how to use them well. Now, who is your mother?'

'My mother?' asked the boy, confused by the sudden transition. 'My mother is staff nurse Masemola.'

'Ao!' exclaimed the prophetess. 'You are the son of the nurse? Does she have such a big man now?' She smiled a little and the lip circle opened. She smiled like a pretty woman who did not want to expose her cavities.

The boy relaxed somewhat, vaguely feeling safe because the prophetess knew his mother. This made him look away from the prophetess for a while, and he saw that there was a huge mask on the wall just opposite her. It was shining and black. It grinned all the time showing two canine teeth pointing upwards. About ten feet away at the other side of the wall was a picture of Jesus in which His chest was open, revealing His heart which had many shafts of light radiating from it.

'Your mother has a heart of gold, my son,' continued the prophetess. 'You are very fortunate, indeed, to have such a parent. Remember, when she says, "My boy, take this message to that house," go. When she says, "My boy, let me send you to the shop," go. And when she says, "My boy, pick up a book and read," pick up a book and read. In all this she is actually saying to you, learn and serve. Those two things, little man, are the greatest inheritance.'

Then the prophetess looked up at the bamboo cross as if she saw something in it that the boy could not see. She seemed to lose her breath for a while. She coughed deeply again, after which she went silent, her cheeks moving as if she was chewing.

'Bring the bottle nearer,' she said finally. She put one hand on the bottle while with the other she held the bamboo cross. Her eyes closed, she turned her face towards the ceiling. The boy saw that her face seemed to have contracted into an intense concentration in such a way that the wrinkles seemed to have become deep gorges. Then she began to speak.

'You will not know this hymn, boy, so listen. Always listen to new things. Then try to create too. Just as I have learnt never to page through the dead leaves of hymn books.' And she began to sing.

> If the fish in a river
> boiled by the midday sun
> can wait for the coming of evening,
> we too can wait
> in this wind-frosted land,
> the spring will come,
> the spring will come.
> If the reeds in winter
> can dry up and seem dead
> and then rise
> in the spring,
> we too will survive the fire that is
> coming
> the fire that is coming,
> we too will survive the fire that is
> coming.

It was a long, slow song. Slowly, the prophetess began to pray.

'God, the All Powerful! When called upon, You always listen. We direct our hearts and thoughts to You. How else could it be? There is so much evil in the world; so much emptiness in our hearts; so much debasement of the mind. But You, God of all power, are the wind that sweeps away evil and fills our hearts and minds with renewed strength and hope. Remember Samson? Of course You do, O Lord. You created him, You, maker of all things. You brought him out of a barren woman's womb, and since then, we have known that out of the desert things will grow, and that what grows out of the barren wastes has a strength that can never be destroyed.'

Suddenly, the candle flame went down. The light seemed to have gone into retreat as the darkness loomed out, seemingly out of the very light itself, and bore down upon it, until there was a tiny blue flame on the table looking so vulnerable and so strong at the same time. The boy shuddered and felt the coldness of the floor going up his bare feet.

Then out of the dark, came the prophetess's laugh. It began as a giggle, the kind the girls would make when the boy and his friends chased them down the street for a little kiss. The giggle broke into the kind of laughter that produced tears when one was very happy. There was a kind of strange pleasurable rhythm to it that gave the boy a momentary enjoyment of the dark, but the laugh gave way to a long shriek. The boy wanted to rush out of the house. But something strong, yet intangible, held him fast to where he was. It was probably the shriek itself that had filled the dark room and now seemed to come out of the mask on the wall. The boy felt like throwing himself on the floor to wriggle and roll like a snake until he became tired and fell into a long sleep at the end of which would be the kind of bliss the boy would feel when he was happy and his mother was happy and she embraced him, so closely.

But the giggle, the laugh, the shriek, all ended as abruptly as they had started as the darkness swiftly receded from the candle like the way ripples run away from where a stone has been thrown in the water. And there was light. On the wall, the mask smiled silently, and the heart of Jesus sent out yellow light.

'Lord, Lord, Lord,' said the prophetess slowly in a quiet, surprisingly full voice which carried the same kind of contentment that had been in the voice of the boy's mother when one day he had come home from playing in the street, and she was seated on the chair close to the kitchen door, just opposite the warm stove. And as soon as she saw him come in, she embraced him all the while saying: 'I've been so ill; for so long, but I've got you. You're my son. You're my son. You're my son.'

And the boy had smelled the faint smell of camphor on her, and he too embraced her, holding her firmly although his arms could not go beyond his mother's armpits. He remembered how warm his hands had become in her armpits.

'Lord, Lord, Lord,' continued the prophetess, 'have mercy on the desert in our hearts and in our thoughts. Have mercy. Bless this water; fill it with your power; and may it bring rebirth. Let her and all others who will drink of it feel the flower of newness spring alive in them; let those who drink it, break the chains of despair, and may they realise that the desert wastes are really not barren, but that the vast sands that stretch into the horizon are the measure of the seed in us.'

As the prophetess stopped speaking, she slowly lowered the bamboo cross until it rested on the floor. The boy wondered if it was all over now. Should he stand up and get the blessed water and leave? But the prophetess soon gave him direction.

'Come here, my son,' she said, 'and kneel before me here.' The boy stood up and walked slowly towards the prophetess. He knelt on the floor, his hands hanging at his sides. The prophetess placed her hands on his head. They were warm, and the warmth seemed to go through his hair, penetrating deep through his scalp into the very centre of his head. Perhaps, he thought, that was the soul of the prophetess going into him. Wasn't it said that when the prophetess placed her hands on a person's head, she was seeing with her soul deep into that person; that, as a result, the prophetess could never be deceived? And the boy wondered how his lungs looked to her. Did she see the water that he had drunk from the tap just across the street? Where was the water now? In the stomach? In the kidneys?

Then the hands of the prophetess moved all over the boy's head, seeming to feel for something. They went down the neck. They seemed cooler now, and the coolness seemed to tickle the boy for his neck was colder than those hands. Now they covered his face, and he saw, just before he closed his eyes, the skin folds on the hands so close to his eyes that they looked like many mountains. Those hands smelled of blue soap and candle wax. But there was no smell of snuff. The boy wondered. Perhaps the prophetess did not use snuff after all. But the boy's grandmother did, and her hands always smelled of snuff. Then the prophetess spoke.

'My son,' she said, 'we are made of all that is in the world. Go. Go and heal your mother.' When she removed her hands from the boy's face, he felt his face grow cold, and there was a slight sensation of his skin shrinking. He rose from the floor, lifted the bottle with its snout, and backed away from the prophetess. He then turned and walked towards the door. As he closed it, he saw the prophetess shuffling away to the bedroom carrying the candle with her. He wondered when she would return the ashtray to the table. When he finally closed the door, the living room was dark, and there was light in the bedroom.

It was night outside. The boy stood on the veranda for a while, wanting his eyes to adjust to the darkness. He wondered also about the dog. But it did not seem to be around. And there was that vine archway with its forbidden fruit and the multicoloured worms that always crawled all over the vine. As the boy walked under the tunnel of vine, he tensed his neck, lowering his head as people do when walking in the rain. He was anticipating the reflex action of shaking off a falling worm. Those worms were disgustingly huge, he thought. And there was also something terrifying about their bright colours.

In the middle of the tunnel, the boy broke into a run and was out of the gate: free. He thought of his mother waiting for the holy water; and he broke into a sprint, running west up Thipe Street towards home. As he got to the end of the street, he heard the hum of the noise that came from the ever-crowded barber shops and the huge beer hall just behind those shops. After the brief retreat in the house of the prophetess, the noise, the people, the shops, the street lights, the buses and the taxis all seemed new. Yet, somehow, he wanted to avoid any contact with all this activity. If he turned left at the corner, he would have to go past the shops into the lit Moshoeshoe Street and its Friday night crowds. If he went right, he would have to go past the now dark, ghostly Bantu-Batho post office, and then down through the huge gum trees behind the Charterston Clinic, and then past the quiet golf course. The latter way would be faster, but too dark and dangerous for a mere boy, even with the spirit of the prophetess in him. And were not dead bodies found there sometimes? The boy turned left.

At the shops, the boy slowed down to manoeuvre through the crowds. He lifted the bottle to his chest and supported it from below with the other hand. He must hold on to that bottle. He was going to heal his mother. He tightened the bottle cap. Not a drop was to be lost. The boy passed the shops.

Under a street lamp just a few feet from the gate into the beer hall was a gang of boys standing in a tight circle. The boy slowed down to an anxious stroll. Who were they? he wondered. He would have to run past them quickly. No, there would be no need. He recognised Timi and Bubu. They were with the rest of the gang from the boy's neighbourhood. Those were the bigger boys who were either in Standard Six or were already in secondary school or were now working in town.

Timi recognised the boy.

'Ja, sonny boy,' greeted Timi. 'What's a picaninny like you doing alone in the streets at night?'

'*Heit*, bra Timi,' said the boy, returning the greeting. 'Just from the shops, bra Timi,' he lied, not wanting to reveal his real mission. Somehow that would not have been appropriate.

'Come on, you!' yelled another member of the gang, glaring at Timi. It was Biza. Most of the times when the boy had seen Biza, the latter was stopping a girl and talking to her. Sometimes the girl would laugh. Sometimes Biza would twist her arm until she 'agreed'. In broad daylight!

'You don't believe me,' continued Biza to Timi, 'and when I try to show you some proof you turn away to greet an ant.'

'Okay then,' said another, 'what proof do you have? Everybody knows that Sonto is a hard girl to get.'

'Come closer then,' said Biza, 'and I'll show you.' The boy was closed out of the circle as the gang closed in towards Biza, who was at the centre. The boy became curious and got closer. The wall was impenetrable. But he could clearly hear Biza.

'You see? You can all see. I've just come from that girl. Look! See? The liquid? See? When I touch it with my finger and then leave it, it follows like a spider's web.'

'Well, my man,' said someone, 'you can't deceive anybody with that. It's the usual trick. A fellow just blows his nose and then applies the mucus there, and then emerges out of the dark saying he has just had a girl.'

'Let's look again closely,' said another, 'before we decide one way or the other.' And the gang pressed close again.

'You see? You see?' Biza kept saying.

'I think Biza has had that girl,' said someone.

'It's mucus, man, and nothing else,' said another.

'But you know Biza's record in these matters, gents.'

'Another thing, how do we know it's Sonto and not some other girl? Where is it written on Biza's cigar that he has just had Sonto? Show me where it's written "Sonto" there.'

'You're jealous, you guys, that's your problem,' said Biza. The circle went loose and there was just enough time for the boy to see Biza's penis disappear into his trousers. A thick little thing, thought the boy.

It looked sad. It had first been squeezed in retreat against the fly like a concertina, before it finally disappeared. Then Biza, with a twitch of alarm across his face, saw the boy.

'What did you see, you?' screamed Biza. 'Fuck off!'

The boy took to his heels wondering what Biza could have been doing with his penis under the street lamp. It was funny, whatever it was. It was silly too. Sinful. The boy was glad that he had got the holy water away from those boys and that none of them had touched the bottle.

And the teachers were right, thought the boy. Silliness was all those boys knew. And then they would go to school and fail test after test. Silliness and school did not go together.

The boy felt strangely superior. He had the power of the prophetess in him. And he was going to pass that power to his mother, and heal her. Those boys were not healing their mothers. They just left their mothers alone at home. The boy increased his speed. He had to get home quickly. He turned right at the charge office and sped towards the clinic. He crossed the road that went to town and entered Mayaba Street. Mayaba Street was dark and the boy could not see. But he did not lower his speed. Home was near now, instinct would take him there. His eyes would adjust to the darkness as he raced along. He lowered the bottle from his chest and let it hang at his side, like a pendulum that was not moving. He looked up at the sky as if light would come from the stars high up to lead him home. But when he lowered his face, he saw something suddenly loom before him, and, almost simultaneously, felt a dull yet painful impact against his thigh. Then there was a grating of metal seeming to scoop up sand from the street. The boy did not remember how he fell but, on the ground, he lay clutching at his painful thigh. A few feet away, a man groaned and cursed.

'Blasted child!' he shouted. 'Shouldn't I kick you? Just running in the street as if you owned it. Shit of a child, you don't even pay tax. Fuck off home before I do more damage to you!' The man lifted his bicycle, and the boy saw him straightening the handles. And the man rode away.

The boy raised himself from the ground and began to limp home, conscious of nothing but the pain in his thigh. But it was not long before he felt a jab of pain at the centre of his chest and his heart beating faster. He was thinking of the broken bottle and the spilt holy water and his mother waiting for him and the water that would help to cure her. What would his mother say? If only he had not stopped to see those silly boys he might not have been run over by a bicycle. Should he go back to the prophetess? No. There was the dog, there was the vine, there were the worms. There was the prophetess herself. She would not let anyone who wasted her prayers get away without punishment. Would it be lightning? Would it be the fire of hell? What would it be? The boy limped home to face his mother. He would walk in to his doom. He would walk into his mother's bedroom, carrying no cure, and face the pain in her sad eyes.

But as the boy entered the yard of his home, he heard the sound of bottles coming from where his dog had its kennel. Rex had jumped over the bottles, knocking some stones against them in his rush to meet the boy. And the boy remembered the pile of bottles next to the kennel. He felt grateful as he embraced the dog. He selected a bottle from the heap. Calmly, as if he had known all the time what he would do in such a situation, the boy walked out of the yard again, towards the street tap on Mayaba Street. And there, almost mechanically, he cleaned the bottle, shaking it many times with clean water. Finally, he filled it with water and wiped its outside clean against his trousers. He tightened the cap and limped home.

As soon as he opened the door, he heard his mother's voice in the bedroom. It seemed some visitors had come while he was away.

'I'm telling you, *Sisi*,' his mother was saying, 'and take it from me, a trained nurse. Pills, medicines, and all those injections, are not enough. I take herbs too, and then think of the wonders of the universe as our people have always done. Son, is that you?'

'Yes, Ma,' said the boy who had just closed the door with a deliberate bang.

'And did you bring the water?'

'Yes, Ma.'

'Good. I knew you would. Bring the water and three cups. MaShange and MaMokoena are here.'

The boy's eyes misted with tears. His mother's trust in him: would he repay it with such dishonesty? He would have to be calm. He wiped his eyes with the back of his hand, and then put the bottle and three cups on a tray. He would have to walk straight. He would have to hide the pain in his thigh. He would have to smile at his mother. He would have to smile at the visitors. He picked up the tray; but just before he entered the passage leading to the bedroom, he stopped, trying to muster courage. The voices of the women in the bedroom reached him clearly.

'I hear you very well, Nurse,' said one of the women. 'It is that kind of sense I was trying to spread before the minds of these people. You see, the two children are first cousins. The same blood runs through them.'

'That close!' exclaimed the boy's mother.

'Yes, that close. MaMokoena here can bear me out; I told them in her presence. Tell the nurse, you were there.'

'I have never seen such people in all my life,' affirmed MaMokoena.

'So I say to them, my voice reaching up to the ceiling, "Hey, you people, I have seen many years. If these two children really want to marry each other, then a beast *has* to be slaughtered to cancel the ties of blood . . ."'

'And do you want to hear what they said?' interrupted MaMokoena.

'I'm listening with both ears,' said the boy's mother.

'Tell her, child of Shange,' said MaMokoena.

'They said that was old, crusted foolishness. So I said to myself, "Daughter of Shange, shut your mouth, sit back, open your eyes, and watch." And that's what I did.

'Two weeks before the marriage, the ancestors struck. Just as I had thought. The girl had to be rushed to hospital, her legs swollen like trousers full of air on the washing line. Then I got my chance, and opened my mouth, pointing my finger at them, and said, "Did you ask the ancestors' permission for this unacceptable marriage?" You should have seen their necks becoming as flexible as a goose's. They looked this way, and looked that way, but never at me. But my words had sunk. And before the sun went down, we were eating the insides of a goat. A week later, the children walked up to the altar. And the priest said to them, "You are such beautiful children!"'

'Isn't it terrible that some people just let misfortune fall upon them?' remarked the boy's mother.

'Only those who ignore the words of the world speaking to them,' said MaShange.

'Where is this boy now?' said the boy's mother. 'Son! Is the water coming?'

Instinctively the boy looked down at his legs. Would the pain in his thigh lead to the swelling of his legs? Or would it be because of his deception? A tremor of fear went through him; but he had to control it, and be steady, or the bottle of water would topple over. He stepped forward into the passage. There was his mother! Her bed faced the passage, and he had seen her as soon as he turned into the passage. She had propped herself up with many pillows. Their eyes met, and she smiled, showing the gap in her upper front teeth that she liked to poke her tongue into. She wore a fawn chiffon *doek* which had slanted into a careless heap on one side of her head. This exposed her undone hair on the other side of her head.

As the boy entered the bedroom, he smelled camphor. He greeted the two visitors and noticed that, although it was warm in the bedroom, MaShange, whom he knew, wore her huge, heavy, black, and shining overcoat. MaMokoena had a blanket over her shoulders. Their *doeks* were more orderly than the boy's mother's. The boy placed the tray on the dressing chest close to his mother's bed. He stepped back and watched his mother, not sure whether he should go back to the kitchen, or wait to meet his doom.

'I don't know what I would do without this boy,' said the mother as she leaned on an elbow, lifted the bottle with the other hand, and turned the cap rather laboriously with the hand on whose elbow she was resting. The boy wanted to help, but he felt he couldn't move. The mother poured water into one cup, drank from it briefly, turned her face towards the ceiling, and closed her eyes. 'Such cool water!' she sighed deeply, and added, 'Now I can pour for you,' as she poured water into the other two cups.

There was such a glow of warmth in the boy as he watched his mother, so much gladness in him that he forgave himself. What had the prophetess seen in him? Did she still feel him in her hands? Did she know what he had just done? Did holy water taste any differently from ordinary water? His mother didn't seem to find any difference. Would she be healed?

'As we drink the prophetess's water,' said MaShange, 'we want to say how grateful we are that we came to see for ourselves how you are.'

'I think I feel better already. This water, and you . . . I can feel a soothing coolness deep down.'

As the boy slowly went out of the bedroom, he felt the pain in his leg, and felt grateful. He had healed his mother. He would heal her tomorrow, and always with all the water in the world. He had healed her.

NADINE GORDIMER

Amnesty

When we heard he was released I ran all over the farm and through the fence to our people on the next farm to tell everybody. I only saw afterwards I'd torn my dress on the barbed wire, and there was a scratch, with blood, on my shoulder.

He went away from this place eight years ago, signed up to work in town with what they call a construction company – building glass walls up to the sky. For the first two years he came home for the weekend once a month and two weeks at Christmas; that was when he asked my father for me. And he began to pay. He and I thought that in three years he would have paid enough for us to get married. But then he started wearing that T-shirt, he told us he'd joined the union, he told us about the strike, how he was one of the men who went to talk to the bosses because some others had been laid off after the strike. He's always been good at talking, even in English – he was the best at the farm school, he used to read the newspapers the Indian wraps soap and sugar in when you buy at the store.

There was trouble at the hostel where he had a bed, and riots over paying rent in the townships and he told me – just me, not the old ones – that wherever people were fighting against the way we are treated they were doing it for all of us, on the farms as well as the towns, and the unions were with them, he was with them, making speeches, marching. The third year, we heard he was in prison. Instead of getting married. We didn't know where to find him, until he went on trial. The case was heard in a town far away. I couldn't go often to the court because by that time I had passed my Standard 8 and I was working in the farm school. Also my parents were short of money. Two of my brothers who had gone away to work in town didn't send home; I suppose they lived with girlfriends and had to buy things for them. My father and other brother work here for the Boer and the pay is very small, we have two goats, a few cows we're allowed to graze, and a patch of land where my mother can grow vegetables. No cash from that.

When I saw him in the court he looked beautiful in a blue suit with a striped shirt and brown tie. All the accused – his comrades, he said – were well dressed. The union bought the clothes so that the judge and the prosecutor would know they weren't dealing with stupid yes-baas black men who didn't know their rights. These things and everything else about the court and trial he explained to me when I was allowed to visit him in jail. Our little girl was born while the trial went on and when I brought the baby to court the first time to show him, his comrades hugged him and then hugged me across the barrier of the prisoners' dock and they had clubbed together to give me some money as a present for the baby. He chose the name for her, Inkululeko.

Then the trial was over and he got six years. He was sent to the Island. We all knew about the Island. Our leaders had been there so long. But I have never seen the sea except to colour it in blue at school, and I couldn't imagine a piece of earth surrounded by it. I could only think of a cake of dung, dropped by the cattle, floating in a pool of rainwater they'd crossed, the water showing the sky like a looking-glass, blue. I was ashamed only to think that. He had told me how the glass walls showed the pavement trees and the other buildings in the street and the colours of the cars and the clouds as the crane lifted him on a platform higher and higher through the sky to work at the top of a building.

He was allowed one letter a month. It was my letter because his parents didn't know how to write. I used to go to them where they worked on another farm to ask what message they wanted to send. The mother always cried and put her hands on her head and said nothing, and the old man, who preached to us in the veld every Sunday, said tell my son we are praying, God will make everything all right for him. Once he wrote back, That's the trouble – our people on the farms, they're told God will decide what's good for them so that they won't find the force to do anything to change their lives.

After two years had passed, we – his parents and I – had saved up enough money to go to Cape Town to visit him. We went by train and slept on the floor at the station and asked the way, next day, to the ferry. People were kind; they all knew that if you wanted the ferry it was because you had somebody of yours on the Island.

And there it was – there was the sea. It was green *and* blue, climbing and falling, bursting white, all the way to the sky. A terrible wind was slapping it this way and that; it hid the Island, but people like us, also waiting for the ferry, pointed where the Island must be, far out in the sea that I never thought would be like it really was.

There were other boats, and ships as big as buildings that go to other places, all over the world, but the ferry is only for the Island, it doesn't go anywhere else in the world, only to the Island. So everybody waiting there was waiting for the Island, there could be no mistake we were not in the right place. We had sweets and biscuits, trousers and a warm coat for him (a woman standing with us said we wouldn't be allowed to give him the clothes) and I wasn't wearing, any more, the old beret pulled down over my head that farm girls wear, I had bought relaxer cream from the man who comes round the farms selling things out of a box on his bicycle, and my hair was combed up thick under a flowered scarf that didn't cover the gold-coloured rings in my ears. His mother had her blanket tied round her waist over her dress, a farm woman, but I looked just as good as any of the other girls there. When the ferry was ready to take us, we stood all pressed together and quiet like the cattle waiting to be let through a gate. One man kept looking round with his chin moving up and down, he was counting, he must have been afraid there were too many to get on and he didn't want to be left behind. We all moved up to the policeman in charge and everyone ahead of us went on to the boat. But when our turn came and he put out his hand for something, I didn't know what.

We didn't have a permit. We didn't know that before you come to Cape Town, before you come to the ferry for the Island, you have to have a police permit to visit a prisoner on the Island. I tried to ask him nicely. The wind blew the voice out of my mouth.

We were turned away. We saw the ferry rock, bumping the landing where we stood, moving, lifted and dropped by all that water, getting smaller and smaller until we didn't know if we were really seeing it or one of the birds that looked black, dipping up and down, out there.

The only good thing was one of the other people took the sweets and biscuits for him. He wrote and said he got them. But it wasn't a good letter. Of course not. He was cross with me; I should have found out, I should have known about the permit. He was right – I bought the train tickets, I asked where to go for the ferry, I should have known about the permit. I have passed Standard 8. There was an advice office to go to in town, the churches ran it, he wrote. But the farm is so far from town, we on the farms don't know about these things. It was as he said; our ignorance is the way we are kept down, this ignorance must go.

We took the train back and we never went to the Island – never saw him in the three more years he was there. Not once. We couldn't find the money for the train. His father died and I had to help his mother from my pay. For our people the worry is always money, I wrote. When will we ever have money? Then he sent such a good letter. That's what I'm on the Island for, far away from you, I'm here so that one day our people will have the things they need, land, food, the end of ignorance. There was something else – I could just read the word 'power' the prison had blacked out. All his letters were not just for me; the prison officer read them before I could.

•

He was coming home after only five years!

That's what it seemed to me, when I heard – the five years was suddenly disappeared – nothing! – there was no whole year still to wait. I showed my – our – little girl his photo again. That's your daddy, he's coming, you're going to see him. She told the other children at school, I've got a daddy, just as she showed off about the kid goat she had at home.

We wanted him to come at once, and at the same time we wanted time to prepare. His mother lived with one of his uncles; now that his father was dead there was no house of his father for him to take me to as soon as we married. If there had been time, my father would have cut poles, my mother and I would have baked bricks, cut thatch, and built a house for him and me and the child.

We were not sure what day he would arrive. We only heard on my radio his name and the names of some others who were released. Then at the Indian's store I noticed the newspaper, *The Nation*, written by black people, and on the front a picture of a lot of people dancing and waving – I saw at once it was at that ferry. Some men were being carried on other men's shoulders. I couldn't see which one was him. We were waiting. The ferry had brought him from the Island but we remembered Cape Town is a long way from us. Then he did come. On a Saturday, no school, so I was working with my mother, hoeing and weeding round the pumpkins and mealies, my hair, that I meant to keep nice, tied in an old *doek*. A combi came over the veld and his comrades had brought him. I wanted to run away and wash but he stood there stretching his legs, calling, hey! hey! with his comrades making a noise around him, and my mother started shrieking in the old style aie! aie! and my father was clapping and stamping towards him. He held his arms open to us, this big man in town clothes, polished shoes, and all the time while he hugged me I was holding my dirty hands, full of mud, away from him behind his back. His teeth hit me hard through his lips, he grabbed at my mother and she struggled to hold the child up to him. I thought we would all fall down! Then everyone was quiet. The child hid behind my mother. He picked her up but she turned her head away to her shoulder. He spoke to her gently but she wouldn't speak to him. She's nearly six years old! I told her not to be a baby. She said, That's not him.

The comrades all laughed, we laughed, she ran off and he said, She has to have time to get used to me.

He has put on weight, yes; a lot. You couldn't believe it. He used to be so thin his feet looked too big for him. I used to feel his bones but now – that night – when he lay on me he was so heavy, I didn't remember it was like that. Such a long time. It's strange to get stronger in prison; I thought he wouldn't have enough to eat and would come out weak. Everyone said, Look at him! – he's a man, now. He laughed and banged his fist on his chest, told them how the comrades exercised in their cells, he would run three miles a day, stepping up and down on one place on the floor of that small cell where he was kept. After we were together at night we used to whisper a long time but now I can feel he's thinking of some things I don't know and I can't worry him with talk. Also I don't know what to say. To ask him what it was like, five years shut away there; or to tell him something about school or about the child. What else has happened, here? Nothing. Just waiting.

Sometimes in the daytime I do try to tell him what it was like for me, here at home on the farm, five years. He listens, he's interested, just like he's interested when people from the other farms come to visit and talk to him about little things that happened to them while he was away all that time on the Island. He smiles and nods, asks a couple of questions and then stands up and stretches. I see it's to show them it's enough, his mind is going back to something he was busy with before they came. And we farm people are very slow; we tell things slowly, he used to, too.

He hasn't signed on for another job. But he can't stay at home with us; we thought, after five years over there in the middle of that green and blue sea, so far, he would rest with us a little while. The combi or some car comes to fetch him and he says don't worry, I don't know what day I'll be back. At first I asked, what week, next week? He tried to explain to me: in the Movement it's not like it was in the union, where you do your work every day and after that you are busy with meetings; in the Movement you never know where you will have to go and what is going to come up next. And the same with money. In the Movement, it's not like a job, with regular pay — I know that, he doesn't have to tell me — it's like it was going to the Island, you do it for all our people who suffer because we haven't got money, we haven't got land — look, he said, speaking of my parents', my home, the home that has been waiting for him, with his child: look at this place where the white man owns the ground and lets you squat in mud and tin huts here only as long as you work for him — *Baba* and your brother planting his crops and looking after his cattle, Mama cleaning his house and you in the school without even having the chance to train properly as a teacher. The farmer owns us, he says. I've been thinking we haven't got a home because there wasn't time to build a house before he came from the Island; but we haven't got a home at all. Now I've understood that.

I'm not stupid. When the comrades come to this place in the combi to talk to him here I don't go away with my mother after we've brought them tea or (if she's made it for the weekend) beer. They like her beer, they talk about our culture and there's one of them who makes a point of putting his arm around my mother, calling her the mama of all of them, the mama of Africa. Sometimes they please her very much by telling her how they used to sing on the Island and getting her to sing an old song we all know from our grandmothers. Then they join in with their strong voices. My father doesn't like this noise travelling across the veld; he's afraid that if the Boer finds out my man is a political, from the Island, and he's holding meetings on the Boer's land, he'll tell my father to go, and take his family with him. But my brother says if the Boer asks anything just tell him it's a prayer meeting. Then the singing is over; my mother knows she must go away into the house.

I stay, and listen. He forgets I'm there when he's talking and arguing about something I can see is important, more important than anything we could ever have to say to each other when we're alone. But now and then, when one of the other comrades is speaking I see him look at me for a moment the way I will look up at one of my favourite children in school to encourage the child to understand. The men don't speak to me and I don't speak. One of the things they talk about is organising the people on the farms – the workers, like my father and brother, and like his parents used to be. I learn what all these things are: minimum wage, limitation of working hours, the right to strike, annual leave, accident compensation, pensions, sick and even maternity leave. I am pregnant, at last I have another child inside me, but that's women's business. When they talk about the Big Man, the Old Men, I know who these are: our leaders are also back from prison. I told him about the child coming; he said, And this one belongs to a new country, he'll build the freedom we've fought for! I know he wants to get married but there's no time for that at present. There was hardly time for him to make the child. He comes to me just like he comes here to eat a meal or put on clean clothes. He picks up the little girl and swings her round and there! – it's done, he's getting into the combi, he's already turning to his comrade that face of his that knows only what's inside his head, those eyes that move quickly as if he's chasing something you can't see. The little girl hasn't had time to get used to this man. But I know she'll be proud of him, one day!

How can you tell that to a child six years old? But I tell her about the Big Man and the Old Men, our leaders, so she'll know that her father was with them on the Island, this man is a great man, too.

On Saturday, no school and I plant and weed with my mother, she sings but I don't; I think. On Sunday there's no work, only prayer meetings out of the farmer's way under the trees, and beer drinks at the mud and tin huts where the farmers allow us to squat on their land. I go off on my own as I used to do when I was a child, making up games and talking to myself where no one would hear me or look for me. I sit on a warm stone in the late afternoon, high up, and the whole valley is a path between the hills, leading away from my feet. It's the Boer's farm but that's not true, it belongs to nobody. The cattle don't know that anyone says he owns it, the sheep – they are grey stones, and then they become a thick grey snake moving – don't know. Our huts and the old mulberry tree and the little brown mat of earth that my mother dug over yesterday, way down there, and way over there the clump of trees round the chimneys and the shiny thing that is the TV mast of the farmhouse – they are nothing, on the back of this earth. It could twitch them away like a dog does a fly.

I am up with the clouds. The sun behind me is changing the colours of the sky and the clouds are changing themselves, slowly, slowly. Some are white, blowing themselves up like bubbles. Underneath is a bar of grey, not enough to make rain. It gets longer and darker while the other clouds are all pink, it grows a thin snout and long body and then the end of it is a tail. There's a huge grey rat moving across the sky, eating the sky.

The child remembered the photo; she said, That's not him. I'm sitting here where I came often when he was on the Island. I came to get away from the others, to wait by myself.

I'm watching the rat, it's losing itself, it's shape, eating the sky, and I'm waiting. Waiting for him to come back.

Waiting. I'm waiting to come back home.

LINDIWE MABUZA

Wake . . .

FOR THEM: NAME THIS DAY GRAVE IN JUNE 1976:
FOR HER
NOW AND AFTER
BECAME FOREVER

     i   became aware: wake up to
    ii became conscious: i.e. after sleep
   iii became militant: wake up and fight
    iv vigil for the dead
     v furrow of water following ship

This was funeral day in Soweto. One day was an eternity to forget all other days leading to it. People had emerged to pay their last pretext to it. Respect was no longer spoken of. On such a day everyone has written permission to pretend the dead have always been alive. Yet even the womb of the earth knew by the smells and languages of Johannesburg that every African hand represented charged wires of dead labour.

      Thina Silangazela   (We crave
      Ikhaya Laphezulu   that home above)

   The drums and chorus of the Zion Christian sects competed with pennywhistle cries of reed and rib ingenuity. There was smoke and dust too, even in these early hours, vainly rising and slithering to choke the various hints of township jazz. Thokozile had been first at fat-cake auntie's house. Now, the greased newspaper rested peacefully under the eight-year-old armpit. One would have thought tears had drowned her sight. No! For her greeting this morning was not a child's. 'We see you! Though what's there to see ourselves over.'

For children grow like mushrooms on funeral day. Bullets had spoken on Wednesday. It was Nolwazi's turn to skip rope. 'If only she had not been so fast.'

Thoko kept blaming Lwazi. She should have landed and remained on the ground and then she would not have been caught, in their birdfly style of skipping. Mid-air, head and bullets met. One whizzed, the other dazed, and both landed spent. Thoko had put her thumb in the wound. But Lwazi was dead.

How could she be sure whether it was the blood or the brain she wanted to push back first into her playmate's head? Her hand was overpowered and since no one else noticed the bloody piece of steel drop on her lap, she quickly shoved it back into the entrance, or was it exit? Then she had asked her feet to carry her into the outhouse, fast, to rest from all the openings on Lwazi's head. And the police! Too scared to enter her own house.

●

'Why didn't she answer me?' Thoko had begged herself. 'Why did she look at me like that?' and then
'Lwazi opened her mouth wide but did not say anything. Aah! Sha-a-ame!'

The smell in the toilet was as routine as respect in Johannesburg. Good thing those fat green flies did not mind sharing their home with a runaway child. How brilliantly green the flies! Some buzzed lazily, almost nonchalant since they lacked nothing now. And then she remembered, perhaps vaguely, her mother telling Lwazi and herself how the sheer gloss and sheen green greed blocked blood from moving around the body and then sores spread and began to eat away the health of the whole.

'Awu, this flea! Biting right over the swelling left by its last cousin,' but Thoko was already administering the flea's last bites. She had mastered the art of flea-catching and killing. The best method, one especially recommended for night prowlers, she had learned from

Lwazi. 'First wet your forefinger with saliva. Then roll the finger over the parasite. Then squeeze the parasite. Then place it between your nails and then squirt your blood out of it. Squeeze it all out, dead.' For Thoko and Lwazi the method was guaranteed. Any and all blood-suckers. Their last blood bite.

Sometimes they would give dry runs of the encounter. The imaginary triumphant capture would be punctuated by war dance and stomping manoeuvres and congratulatory embraces. On the podium of friends, levity and games, self-praise was final recommendation. 'Lwazi! She just went down like a bag of corn, *duklu*! thud! Maybe the screams and booms I hear will scare the fly that buzzed over Lwazi's head.'

The flea-catching method did not work with flies though. Lwazi and Thoko had long agreed that they did not especially relish the thought of dissecting the fly's belly, although this would have assured them of necessary extermination of these creatures. Somehow, it never mattered what sex they were. Male or female, flies carried a bag of eggs. No! Squeezing was out of the question. So suffocating them with one of those modern inventions you bought at Moloi's all-purpose store was the most acceptable method of annihilation. With such thoughts rotating faster than the spread-speed of fear, with questions, fleas and flies alternating to colonise her seclusion, Thoko remained on that concrete seat. Or, at the very least, it would be said that with her body slenderised by daily rations of porridge or *mielie* rice, she thinly contained the smell of the place till her mother's voice screamed her out. The mother had thought she would have some rest this night. Factory machines drain. Home is where one gets charged. But now . . . funeral day ahead!

No! respect, not that. There was even winding drummed obstinacy about the word. Every day, but funeral day, black people's respect poured out into white receptacles that greedily soaked up all virtue and tradition except that which rooted whiteness deep into karroos, pla-teaus and the sprawl of the Southern African veld. So why on earth would the word 'respect' even suggest itself when silent graves openly sang praises to the sky that never seems to alter its pattern in spite of its constantly changing colour?

'Oh you of our own,' the sustained sob echoed.

'What have we done on earth?' resounded agonisedly comforting like a funeral orchestra with its invisible strings stretched like a coffin across yawning graves. The chorus is also echoed in the language of clicks and deep hymns where people smile and even chuckle at the awesomeness of dare and death. Condolences.

Live on.

'How many deaths for us, you of our own?' A shrill voice wonders at death's cynicism. Weak from tears and the weight of unanswered questions, many voices danced the staggering steps of a drunkard, shuffling the weary steps of the vigil. They had sat up all night. Thousands of people in different homes. Waiting together for death to teach then as it does everyday in the newspapers. The death toll had reached five hundred. Then no more news! Soon, it would be expensive news. The regime would sell the dead children back to parents. Otherwise? Otherwise!

(*Kutheni na?*	(What happened?
Kutheni na?)	what happened?)
(*Kutheni na?*	(what happened
Kutheni na?)	what happened)
(*Kutheni na?*	(what happened
Kutheni na?)	what happened)
(*Loluhambo?*	(this journey?
Lunengozi . . .)	has danger . . .)

They sang, recounting the tedium of turmoil. They counted on forgetfulness, vainly. They hoped it would deliver them out of the land of pain and dreams. No such relief. At best, not yet! Anger and tiredness had lost appetite. So, the newspaper-wrapped fat-cakes which Thoko had bought just stared, drying themselves out much like the land blighted by droughts.

There was no drama to the eight hundred deaths. No mystery either! Only the quantity and nature of violence. The fascist government wanted Africans to think, breathe, evaluate and conceptualise in Afrikaans. 'Only dogs and slaves are defined by their masters,' said Frederick Douglass. The students said no! to indoctrination and demonstrated. The police shot them. The fascists of South Africa said shoot 'at any cost'. Absolutely no drama to hot pursuit and murder, in cold blood!

Now at Thoko's home, every room was filled to bursting capacity. Even then, in the living room which has now acquired the sadness of a mosque or cathedral were two strips or 'nests' of unoccupied space representing the missing ones.

Please do not feed too long on this emptiness, for your heart could overflow, the silence said. In the valley of life we fear no death. In the valley of death we fear all evil. But where is the cup to receive our precious blood? And in Soweto, people devise ways of drinking sorrow.

The corpses of Thoko's brother and sister wait at a local mortuary. Distance the pain! God! *Molimo*! Things of this earth! When one corpse is one too many it is enough then that nests should tell, as with their books and school uniforms, that the occupants have whirred away. That's just how one felt when they skipped rope, especially in the major league of the sport. They created their unique styles but the envy of all was the birdfly. Thoko and Lwazi were the regional champions by peer acclamation

> *Loluhambo lunengozi:*
> (This journey has danger)
> *Loluhambo lunosizi:*
> (This journey had grief)
> *Kutheni na: Kutheni na?*
> (What happened: what happened?)
> *Kutheni na: Kutheni na?*
> (What happened: what happened?)

'Oh! Our sister, do not trouble yourself. Kumalo will get the slip.'

'Our brother, they burned down the office. We need permission to bury the . . . dead.'

'Yes, yes, our sister. How can I forget? But I also know my brother-by-custom. We wouldn't have married you to a tree. I know him. I swear by those under, he will get that slip.'

'Yes, our brother, hope does not kill.'

'Don't chuck hope away. My brother is a man. He will knock and knock until he sees a crack at Johannesburg City Hall. You'll see. He'll come back. We'll bury them today.'

More tears streamed as Thoko's mother's strength defied the sombre dignity of factory hands and machinist control.

'You know too, our brother. To . . . sit . . . in . . . your . . . nest . . . with pain . . . All right I'll try . . . and . . . hold myself. But . . . there's the thought that 'ears me that . . . the . . . pain . . . will be d . . . ragg . . . ed. Ayi! No! *Mos*! . . . death is better. They have killed *mos*, what else do they want?'

'Sh . . . no, our sister, do not speak like that. Thoko should not hear you . . . you will stumble our last seed.'

'It is well, our brother.'

She took the wide end of her mourner's tunic to empty some of the salt that had tasted her face from their mutual foundation. Fluids and salts that were ministers. Offices and orifices of sweat-pores, nostrils and eyes. She turned back to see him; speaks.

'I will be careful. I will . . . try . . . caution!' 'No, our sister. Not just you. All of us have to be careful of the growing ones.'

And then her body convulsed with the fever of other memories. And more tears scream in her quietly speaking, or trying to.

'*Mos*, you too know how Boers are, our brother. They kill . . . and murder . . . and throw . . . on rubbish . . . dumps . . . with flies like . . . the child . . . of . . . Modise . . . If Naledi's fa . . . no . . . if Kumalo doesn't get the slip perhaps . . . I was thinking . . . that with some zinc together . . . there is . . . no money to take the children to . . . the . . . cold storage . . . I was thinking . . . that with some of the collection . . . we should get nails and some zinc and rope . . . make . . . two cases . . . now I don't know this hiccup . . . I was thinking . . . we could then . . . place . . . the children . . . no . . . the gone ones . . .' She now no longer sees him, she goes on speaking. 'Ha! Naledi! Naledi! Where is Themba? You should look well after your brother. Don't let the other children chop his tail. As long as they don't cause him pain.'

'Oh! Children can be clever. Because the older high school children know that Themba sings well they said: "No, you, Themba, won't be initiated by singing at *msila*'s concert. We graduate you instantly, automatically. Instead of singing, you see, we are very very thirsty. You will have no tail to cut if you quench this thirst. Now, take this fork," they would say, "and bring us some water till this tiny cup is filled." Ha! Ha! Ha! Oh! Children! But you know Themba tried to get a forkful of water. Then he asked for a spoon.

'A spoon? A tail asking for a spoon? *Msila?* Ha! Ha! Ha! Look here, take this other fork, no maybe three. We only do this to you because you are special, we don't usually give more than two forks but you, Themba, you are special! Ha! Ha! Ha! Heh! Heh!' She sees the children, her children, her brothers, the five of them – the first, then fifth. She laughs. She sees her brother, but only for a second. Which brother! She speaks, wondering.

●

'Why do you shake me so, my brother? Oh! The gone ones . . . careful now . . . place them . . . in . . . zinc . . . case . . . wood swallows water . . . then lower . . . lower . . . them into . . . the cold . . . wa . . . te . . . r . . . s . . . of . . . the . . . ri . . . v . . . er . . . near the . . . tr . . . ees.'

And then she wandered, swimming alone, groping, feeling the tip of a wandering finger belonging to one of the unknowns like the Lwazis and the Naledis and the Thembas, and hundreds more. By then, the shrouded woman was out. Almost as cold as the shallow waters of the white tributary that meanders through Soweto. She drifted. For a while her brother was there to receive the tired thoughts into his steel-milled hands. And then to her all was now and forever irrelevant. What have we done? *Kutheni na?* Nearer my God! The fight will continue. All these converged on those in the living room and adjacent rooms; but only as lives from epic, liberatory songs of a nation. They seemed almost like lonely dissimilar vowels (vowels all the same) for concordial agreement.

The lives converged on all those at Thoko's house, many other homes too. They converged on those around the nest, that swollen mound covered with a black sheet, the centre piece of long toil and misery. And now, the mound was ready to dress with its soil all the bleeding wounds. In death, discordance seemed swallowed by grief then pressed into tears. Already, it would appear as though the tears were endless streams although all who really know feared the worse to come and a worst.

There were hundreds of dear ones now only called the 'gone ones'.

The regime thought and thought till it decided 'no mass funeral for victims of Soweto riots'.

'You, too, Kumalo, (Sir) you bury your children one by one. *Sies!*'

●

Kumalo had walked out of the office, a temporary arrangement at City Hall, Johannesburg, South Africa. Market Street, crossed Von Brandis, Eloff, then towards the Smal Street entrance to Park Station. Hardly more than three decades ago, he remembered rickshaw 'boys' in regal peacock splendour; animal power for beaded chariots that can fly pleasure into the leisure of white world tourists. At night these 'boys' dozed while robbers came or did not come! Hardly more than a decade ago he remembered . . . Yes, Park.

●

This is where workers from Botswana, Lesotho, Mozambique, Zimbabwe, and the various insults called bantustans make their debut to the super-exploitation on the African continent for the benefit of other continents.

●

For a while Kumalo transgressed into this 'foreign' world and the warmth that rose and choked that region of the body only endowed the female of the species, the womb, did not strike him as odd. Not at all! He was a man. But he was not afraid of birth of feeling. Especially not on funeral day! And not for a messenger boy! He was not a man . . . ?

●

Funeral day? This was to be extra added attraction to an otherwise dreary existence filled with some monotonous sounds of law pre-occupied Johannesburg. Johannesburg is the mother-child of Soweto. Stranger, don't be alarmed at such an umbilical existence. The reverse of the question would be more appropriate to answer but since a child of 'Soweto' significantly differs from a Johannesburg darling we shall only ask the question direct: Where is Johannesburg without 'Soweto'? If the cemetery suggests itself, blame it on gold deposited below the earth we trample.

How such thoughts pounded the sore head of Kumalo! And more came as the train flashed! Braamfontein flashed! Peace and privacy reigns! Langlaagte flashed! Candy, lumber, clothing and of course gold flashed! Croesus flashed! none bow before the cemetery except the dead and dying and all flashed before the city of jams, jellies, preserves and all the jolly canned stuff! There's no end to the rise of mine dumps. Lonely cablecarts ride their riddle here and there and back and forth, and there are many lores and many a legend hidden at the base of those white hills. New Canada shimmers in the lake as the train swallows more! But a storm rose inside Kumalo as he watched the burning soil of 'White City' and the tears knocked in his throat wanting an exit, but not this time, while the children burn barefoot on the earth . . . Earth, you fatten not!

We fatten and fatten you with youth and brain. But still you're not satisfied! We're never guests when you set your tables. Always you dine and wine, picking our choice cuts, our promises, our children, our leaders. But still, your bossy fingers itch for more and more. Why do it to us? If this be the prize for gold and other things, why not take your anger to those who anchor me to sweat and die for your keeping? For their crowns and jewels my people wear not. Tell me, Earth, why, why me? I do not grow fat and rich! my people do not wreck you, our earth of our forefathers. We only do our Lord's bidding yet you whip with two swords. No! I would still have died with one! Why did you choose my children if you were hungry? Johannesburg gravy has more fat! Oh Earth you fatten not and then they tell me to bury the late ones on Monday. 'No slip,' the note said. They died on Wednesday and the city could not keep them after Friday. Do I have heart and liver to watch my own rot because the government is afraid of many funerals in one day? I would not like to burn bodies like the Indians but maybe ashes could enliven you as well as anything can.

Oh Earth not one but two of them! Now what of our plans to make Naledi, our first child a beacon to new life and light? Earth, the heavens never ask streams or sand or mountains or any of their vast landscapes to speak the language of the scorching sun. To learn in the language of clashing clouds or even to speak in winter with the peaceful lips of the spring moon.

Let me tell you about this Naledi, Earth. Well, my daughter, well she was a woman but she was a man too. Naledi, we called her that because in Sotho it means star. We have the name in Zulu – Nkanyezi – but it sounded nicer in Sotho because her mother was a Sotho girl when I married her. But Naledi, she had her feet firmly rooted in Soweto. Why on earth should she not say no, Johannesburg! No, Pretoria! No, Witbank! Why shouldn't she, Earth? What else does this Afrikaans language hide that my star saw? That's why they killed my children, killed all children! They saw what they were not supposed to see. Slavery. Trickery. Chaining the mind! No! No! No! No! That's not right, man. At fourteen they kill her! Yesterday the wife had these sleeping spells. Naledi's mother is a good woman. If she was there on the street she would have run between the bullets and the children. She always said she would die for the children to live longer and better. No! She'll be all right with my brother-by-custom on her side. She'll rest from any worry. I know my brother.

Then he raised his head; he was stunned. He had missed Phefeni station and was at Dube. That disturbed him. A man ought to measure correctly even when there is death in the family. No! That's being a willow. Weak. No! That's not Naledi's father. He wished himself convinced that it wasn't thinking too long that made him miss his destination. Just to be sure he was correct he was going to think about his Naledi just so that bad luck would know him. But the present was there in the vibrating rhythm of the station. Dube's sulk painted a painful monotony of acute sombreness and loaded sobriety. Quite unusual for Saturday morning when reprieve, though short-lived, tenaciously holds workers, and workers engage in varieties of thanksgivings to themselves and the day. Quite phenomenal for a day, the only one in the week, when most of Soweto workers consciously or unconsciously forget Friday and Monday or whatever broods between. Where are the attires bought, made, borrowed or ritualistically taken from city stores?

This day, domestic workers even managed to borrow without discussion from their employers' wardrobes, the same bosses that reluctantly let them come to 'that Soweto'. 'I'm not against nice things,' Naledi would say. Yes, let me think about her! Hawu! That child! I can almost hear her voice every evening as I returned from

City Deep Gold Mines. She would leave whatever else she was doing and come to me.

> Naledi: *Sawubona Baba*
> (we see you father)
> Kumalo: *Awu Mntungwa, Mbulazi,*
> *wena owadl'umuntu,*
> *umyenga ngendaba*
> (Oh you of the Mntungwas
> defensively pretentious
> You who finished a person
> beguiling him with story)
> We see you Princess of Ours

Naledi: The water for your feet is ready but I must make you a cup of tea first to wash away the thirst of the day and sweat.

●

Naledi would then proceed to the kitchen. Make the tea, place milk and sugar on a tray, bring it over to the living room where I would have taken off my shoes . . .

Naledi: No, father. (So she would always warn in her warm tone, and bright her eyes.) You just rest. I'll do that.

●

After serving the tea she would then go and get the warm water, add salt, place the towel, soap and scrubbing stone next to the bowl, then stick her own foot in just to test it.

●

Naledi: All right *Baba*, careful now when you place the children in.

Kumalo: No, child of the cities, only women's feet are children in Zulu – *abantwana.*

Naledi: If it were not for the stings inside your feet from walking and standing, shifting paper, I would insist my father has children for feet too . . . my brother also . . .

Kumalo:*Qha.* It has no matter: But I know you say it because you like us.

Naledi: Like you, *Baba*? I die of you! Are the thorns coming out?

Kumalo: Awu! It scratches the heart! Are you still learning nicely from Mahau?

Naledi: Badly nice, *Baba*. It is so nice it can't be explained.

Kumalo: School fees almost finished your mother and me this year with two of you in high school now. You must help your brother to be strong and carry himself right so he can do the work.

Naledi: Ha, *Baba*. You do not know Themba. He has already slaughtered his first arithmetic half-year examination. You know what else? He says he will be a chemist, you know.

Kumalo: That too scratches the heart. But where . . . not in this country!

Naledi: Well, teacher Mahau says it is a matter of time before Angola comes to South Africa. I think he means before we do what they did to the elephant tearing up their land. He says we should not stop reaching and climbing and flying high in our thinking. Hayi, it is those below the earth who brought us Mahau. He really treads where they laboured.

Kumalo: No! I like that. I like what he says.

Naledi: (Wiping Kumalo's feet) Now thank me, *Baba*. (She would wait proudly, attentively.)

Kumalo: Abundance is rejected only by a wizard.

Naledi: No, *Baba*, not that one. One that soothes the heart.

Kumalo: Don't tire even tomorrow?

Naledi: No, *Baba*! You know which one I mean.

Kumalo: *Mntungwa mbu* . . . You of the Ntungwas.

Naledi: Not that either. Thank me. Remind me of the hero you see everyday, moving in and out of Johannesburg!

Kumalo: (Feigning sudden illumination: teasingly) Oh . . . that one!

Both: The Rand Gold Storage is the Rand Cold Storage.

•

This is how the ceremony would always end. Kumalo was at the backdoor of his rented house . . . Orlando West.

With most of the grown-ups languishing in the depth of the general and specific character of mass agony, Thoko chose a spot near the kitchen window where she became lost in the enveloping mood. She had brought the fat-cakes as asked. But as with the adults her own appetite for food had deserted, and in its stead was a more rapacious gnawing presence. It was an eight-year-old desire to know the nature and character of death. When she was five, Thoko had been very sick at her grandmother's in Natal. Her grandmother had said the doctor had said the cause was corn-meal sickness. Thoko must have been very sick because one day her grandmother even decided to miss work. But on that same day a man in a postal-house uniform had brought a yellowish-orange envelope. After reading it, Thoko's grandmother had cried and cried so hard Thoko started crying too. Then she heard her grandmother tell the passersby, those who had been attracted to the house by the sounds, that her grandmother's parents had both died the same day in another part of the country. And then the grandmother would call them: '*Mama We! Awu Baba*'. They were not in the house when she called. They had not walked in as called people usually do. So where did they go? Thoko asked herself. Thoko's corn-meal pains were back as if to claim their portion from her reservoir of weakness and tears. She was still crying that evening when her grandmother, all in black, went to the train station, leaving Thoko with auntie Rose, a niece of Thoko's grandmother. Death, she thought, must be big like the bishop or someone very high up for her grandmother to have to leave her sick like that. Her gogo had left so . . . so . . .

On funeral day, as she sat by the window, her head supported by the cupped hand, she wondered about death. Where did he live and what mansions did he possess to want to claim so many people, also so many people whom she knew, all at once? She suspected how serious death was this day because even though all those adults saw her sitting there 'like an orphan' – as they referred to that posture – no one actually reprimanded her for 'wishing marvel' or motioning to death, sitting in a posture that was a premonition of his coming.

Tears are not always letters, clearly spelling mysteries, yet even to Thoko, death tears did suggest that it was also much better to know

the exact and real source and character of death. This day Thoko's
mother had discreetly taken her hand, then she tried again to explain
the death phenomenon. As on other occasions since that indelible
Wednesday, Thoko's mother had not gone beyond 'It is like ha . . . v
. . . ing . . . a . . . long . . . s . . . l . . . e . . . e . . . p' and then tears
poured down her black dress.

Back by the window Thoko had even wished a long deep sleep. You
can see lots of things other people don't know about when you are in a
long sleep. It happened with Thoko in the lavatory when she hid
herself after she saw the openings on Lwazi's head. Since then, sleep,
like appetite, seemed to prefer other people. Perhaps in other regions
too. Everyone around now seemed to have found it hard to fall asleep,
but then it could be because they were busy singing and praying and
explaining over and over again how it all happened. Each time a
mourner or sets of mourners came, the story of the late ones' death
would be told. But before this abandonment by sleep, Thoko had fallen
asleep in the lavatory after contemplating those green flies and fleas.
Somewhere, between the worrying and the scratching, her thoughts
flew and the long sleep came! And now, she remembered one late
summer afternoon. Naledi was cooking supper. Thoko and Lwazi were
sitting near that same window through which Thoko was now reading
her thoughts. The two girls had been hurried back by an imminent
storm. From the whirling up of any lightfooted object by the boisterous
wind! From a fairly balanced exchange: the sudden sharp blindness of
the splitting lights, thrilling, shivery and shrill, and the raucous roaring
voice of shouting thunder! Thoko and Lwazi agreed, as they had no
other serious questions, that this time without any doubt God in heaven
must be beating up his wife navy-blue. Maybe other women up there
have jumped on him and anyone watching the fight must see what
colour 'bloomers' they are wearing and maybe someone does not have
any on and everyone hides their one eye!

'Haw! Haw! Haw! Haw! Haw!' Seeing. Laughing. Not seeing. And
perhaps in self-defence God's wife must have responded by sending
flying and flaming any tangible missile in sight such as saucers and
cups, a process guaranteed to produce lightning results. Then the first
large tears spat on the window panes; they were accompanied by hail.

As great friends and speculators as the two girls were, they had not yet arrived at any adequate explanation of what caused those rocks. As in any other field of endeavour, our experts tried to give us some light in this domain. Suffice it to say that perhaps the conclusion tolerated by both Lwazi and Thoko derived from subjective reasoning based on observing objective natural reality. When nature is not as happy with the world, winter comes to spread frost on grass and sometimes to bite little fingers and toes. It would seem quite reasonable, then, that the anger of heaven's occupants would produce something more formidable than frost, something that can knock down a head, certainly a superior part of the human anatomy. Allowing for a reasonable suspension of disbelief, should it not follow then that our budding scientists concluded:

If the godheads had proclaimed their anger in a riotous manner, there was plenty of cold debris from that general commotion. Even some of the belchings of the thunder said that. There was cleaning up being done up in heaven. And now what else was earth if not the dumping ground for the most high refuse. They had even heard something akin to this idea in Sunday School. The young lady guest teacher, or was it the young guest lady teacher, from the United States of America, North America, Universe, had taught that after Angel Lucifer fell, God cleaned heaven by sending him and his kith and kin down to earth where he prowls in daily darkness seeking whom he may devour. In their own language, Thoko and Lwazi read it all to mean that what is broken up in God's household can only come down to the ground. It was always cold when their parents quarrelled over money or food.

As they now sat by the window, they spoke of how they could use God's debris by stringing those glassy rocks together and making themselves two diamond necklaces. Yes, Lwazi's father's second brother (Lwazi had never met him) worked in a place where they dig diamonds. Her mother had even shown Lwazi what a watch looks like when its face was the only part that was not diamond: Even the band? And her mother had also shown her rings with lots and lots of these things she called stones. Sometimes on her day-offs Lwazi's mother would just quietly borrow some of Mrs Epstein's jewellery. So Lwazi and Thoko would wear their diamonds in miner uncle Jones's honour and for all the domestic workers like Lwazi's mother. In anticipation, they would even try to walk like any Mrs: bodies thrown forward by high heels, a dog on a leash. 'C'mon, Sport' and 'Sweet boy, c'mon,' their thick lips tightly bundled in the manner of sophisticated Europe speaking and their little torsos perched, they would transform themselves into live white ladies. Happier moments they couldn't imagine.

●

Lwazi: Mrs Pom-Pom my dear shwe shwe shwe shwe! Shwee shwee.

Thoko: My dear Mrs Boom-Boom twee twee twee twee and then twee twee twee twee really?

Afterwards this hilarity filled the kitchen, with Naledi joining in the young ladies' free happiness. On the diamond necklace Naledi intervened though, warning them against the short lifespan of hail, especially against skin warmed by the sun of Africa. They listened and understood. They could always be what they wish.

They listened. They understood.

They could still be Mrs Pom-Pom and Mrs Boom-Boom if they wished. It's just that they really preferred being Thoko's mother, always working with machines, or even making these machines. For her part Naledi told them she was perfectly happy being her father's daughter. Looking straight at the younger girls she firmed her narrowing eyes, imitating the manner of her father! 'It is not wrong to fight for justice,' and then she would go back to her cooking and leave the little ones alone to ponder that for a while.

●

Lwazi: Thoko, would you fight?

Thoko: Depends.

Lwazi: Depends on what?

Thoko: On why I was fighting.

Lwazi: Say, somebody always 'starts' you so that you get angry.

Thoko: Well sometimes my cousin who is a year older than myself 'starts' me by calling me 'baby lion' and then when I get hot I want to fight him. But my mother says that that's not starting me. It is 'teasing for love'. That's what she calls it. Hm . . . I suppose it depends too on who I'm fighting.

Lwazi: But that is good . . . baby lion. Well, now . . . you know, you haven't answered me. Now let's say . . . maybe . . . let's say you were fighting the FL.

Both: EAS. Fleas: Haa. Haa. Haa. Haa. Haa. Haa.

Thoko: Look, Lwazi. Even the rain is fighting.

Lwazi: No, I don't think it's fighting. Maybe it's crying. Haven't you seen your mother scrubbing floors? Well, it is not exactly the same but something close to it. When Ma scrubs the floors she cries tears to help her wash everything clean. Heaven must be throwing away the tears they thought they would use but . . .

Thoko: But I don't understand that at all.

Lwazi: You should remember, Thoko, that heaven is not dirty at all. So, if there was a fight up there followed by the cleaning up and Naledi said our necklaces would melt because the skin is warm, maybe God and his wife are warm and too hot and are laughing tears.

●

Strangely, it begins to dawn.

●

Thoko: Ahaa! And perhaps the broken things that didn't get thrown down as hail just began to melt?

Lwazi: I think so. Now you see. The hail just melts in all that warmness above and it comes straight to us.

●

Now a sense of challenge.

●

Thoko: Ha! How do you know all this?

•

Lwazi: Because they named me Nolwazi. That's how I know. Do you know what Nolwazi means?

Thoko: (Feeling a little shamed) Huh? Well . . . No!

Lwazi: Many people do not know. It means I'm mother of Ukwazi (knowledge) nokuhlakanipha (wisdom).

Thoko: Hey! You are happy.

Lwazi: Why do you say that?

Thoko: Because mine does not say that.

Lwazi: Ya! What does it say? Thoko. What does it mean? Something good, I'm sure.

Thoko: Thoko is really not my whole name. My name is Thokozile.

Lwazi: Mmmmm, Thokozile.

Thoko: Yes! Sithokozile! We are happy. My parents were happy when I arrived.

Lwazi: Does it mean they did not mind? They mind and then they don't. Am I saying it Thokozile?

•

A little song.

•

Thoko: Thoko. Thoko. Thokozile. Sithokozile (We are rejoicing. Our joy is a little lady).

Lomtwana wethu intombi. Hawu Sithokozile.

The song is repeated. Lwazi joins in. Once. Twice. Then again. And again. Now, again, eager to return to her point, not disappointed, pointing:

Thoko: Yes, they didn't mind. But look at those drops in that little pool there. You still don't think they are fighting?

Lwazi: Wooooo! They all want space, fast. (Excitedly, pointedly: the activity in the forming puddle.)

Look, Look!

Thoko: Yes, look how they fight for space. (Satisfied and content to digress). But you don't know why Naledi is Naledi and Themba is Themba.

Lwazi: No, I don't.

Thoko: (Authoritatively, tantalising) Well, do you want to know?

Lwazi: (Sensed dependence) I wouldn't mind. Naledi says information.

Both: Frees:

(Beside herself with wonder and laughter.)

Naledi: Wo! You two are something else. You know . . .

Thoko: Well, Naledi is Naledi, star; and star is right here with us. Now have you ever seen stars cooking? Like this one right now?

(All three laugh).

Lwazi: Not really. No (Indicating with finger on the pane). But I have seen stars die or fall after cooking in the sky. Dwi . . . i . . . i . . . i.

Thoko: Yes! I know that others take their place in the sky. So you know this, Naledi.

Lwazi: Yes! But what about Themba?

Thoko: Themba! Well! Themba is really not his full name. His real name is Thembalethu. It means our hope or the hope of all of us, of the people.

Lwazi: (Now pensive, wondering now) Strange how we get names . . . heh . . . but Thokozile is my best one. It would be nice if we were both Thokozile. We are happy. Or maybe mine should have been Thoko, short for Sothokoza (we will be happy) for the full name.

(Springing back from momentary reverie) Hey! I just remembered. My mother's sister is going to have a baby. She also works in the kitchens. She asked me to give a name for her baby. And whatever name I give, that's what the baby will be called.

Thoko: So what are you thinking?

Lwazi: I'm thinking of naming her baby Sothokoza (we shall rejoice) if it's a boy, or Duma, short for . . .

Thoko: Awu Suka! Why Duma? It could be Dumazile! (we are disappointed)

Lwazi: Because when people use the short form only, Duma, those listening will think it might be the short form of Dumile (famous) or

Dumazulu (Heaven's thunder). I will be happy if it's a baby girl. Nodumo! Mother of renown.

Thoko: Oh! Let's talk about the rain.

Lwazi: All right.

For a good while the two stayed together watching the rain activity through the window pane. As if the icy stones had not been enough confusion, rain drops were now streaming continuously. Before their eyes, the strokes seemed to take positions, each vying for the most advantageous space. For an advent. Venturing. As if those drops that chose to land on clefts or gutters or streams had more results to show for their cumulative collective activity. It was not just Naledi saying it, but they were actually seeing this thing happen. Not too far from the puddle, there was an anthill. Again, Naledi made them watch the difference. It seemed as if those drops that chose to land on that hill could be traced only for a moment furrowing their scattered ways down. But after a while, there would only be furrows left behind and no puddle, Naledi pointed out between cooking and tasting her own creations spiced generously with her mother's artistry born of want. In their own language derived from seeing nature, Thoko and Lwazi articulated the dangers of following the line of least resistance in life.

●

Thoko: Sometimes I don't understand what Sis' Naledi means.

Lwazi: She means that at least we should not be like that all of the time.

Thoko: Like what?

Lwazi: Like soft-soft! weak-weak! Wanting to keep going downhill.

Naledi: Why not? It's easy! And sometimes fun!

Lwazi: Yes, it's easy, but all of the time?

Naledi: Why not? You haven't answered that one yet!

Thoko: Well, because if you keep going downhill all or most of the time, there is no going up.

Naledi: But why? I insist! Why?

(After some silence, and Thoko and Lwazi revealed uneasy smiles.) Because after a while all the paths and space will be . . . ?

Both: They will be for going down!
Naledi: Yes! Thank you!

•

And as time moved faster than life-in-a-dream capsule, Thoko whispered to herself about the two 'goodest' women she knew besides her mother! Lwazi and Naledi. But she was afraid to whisper any further lest her voice should echo too loud like the slightly muffled resonance of flights above the clouds on a rainy day. And she searched for another thought to break the pattering chatter of the roof. (Naledi and Lwazi had disappeared.) The dream remained.

She heard the wagon train but could not see it.

She moved from the seat chilled by her own fears. She moved closer to the window so that Lwazi and Naledi might remember where they left her and would come back for her too. Honest, she would be a good sport! With her face pressed against the window round and flat, flatly round she heard something bounce behind her. She turned around in life pressed round into a dream. She saw the bouncing ball and was afraid. Could it be the void she did not understand, she never thought, never knew! Could it be her mind, the enchanted fairytales or life embodied in a ball? How could one ball keep badgering her, bouncing and laughing? Sometimes it tapped Thoko's shoulder slightly from behind, injecting thoughts that exploded the tongue in the mouth, giving grief the taste of bitterness. She wanted to puncture the poignant bounce out of that hollow tormentor! Oh! But if only she could catch the ball! If only her hand could squeeze it once, much as she has pressed her face against the window pane! Squash it. Squeezing . . . She could do that! Would her hand be too little? And she alone. Alone, she could. But then she remembered, as she followed the bouncing ball, she remembered Naledi telling her and Lwazi that victory could not be as thrilling to a triumphant but closeted wrestler as it would be to a team. No! She did not understand Naledi's sayings sometimes, but that hardly mattered now because the louder and longer she tried to straighten a point the more hysterical the laughter from the ball. She could not absorb and saturate herself with that ridicule, standing and seeming lost in the forest of despair. Never! And still consider herself

Lwazi's friend and Naledi's sister! Never! Her father's protégée too! Never! No more of that. You could see her little strength ascend with each strengthening breath. She was now ready and determined to slice and punch the life out of the demented thrills of the laughing ball that usurped her mind and kitchen space forcing her to follow it right into the open . . . and . . . and then . . . no . . . she could not believe what happened . . . except . . . well! It happened. At precisely her moment of strength the ball bumped the highest it had ever reached. The exalted one! And as it spun down its arrogance exhausted and as always, vulnerable, it dived straight into a puddle where the many drops arrested and swallowed its impetuous elasticity. She moved forward feeling close to the puddle, in her own way. She now wanted nothing more than to rescue this semblance of a ball. But the ball which now seemed like any other tormentor exploded its air, and where it sank, countless happy bubbles emerged with sparkling sounds alternating with the music of raindrops. Thoko wanted to touch these. Slowly, she had to tie it with her will, slowly her hand moved as though it were directed to the gathering forms before her eyes. The rain stopped, completely. And the form grew out of the drying puddle with the intensity and fire of marchers' steps singing from the direction of the river. There was a rainbow of banners and slogans that proudly arched and encored against the spread of the western sunset. She could have sworn that the marchers wore school uniforms. Yet each uniform transformed chameleon-like into a soldier. Thoko's eyes on the marchers, her hand touched the silky silted surface that was the puddle where hundreds of miniature coffins arose all drenched in the colour of earth and blood, earth, blood!

•

Right there on the land of martyrs Lwazi rose from her narrow imprisonment, offering Thoko both her hands. They both looked at the lavatory. Both smiled and then joined their hands, making a bridge and before they could even finish squeezing the pests between their thumb nails, the hundreds of coffins lightly rested on the joined hands. The marchers' song rose like bells at morning break and the bridge and reason for all moved to meet the marchers. Rising to crown the

human rainbow was Naledi's banner, no longer an aloe in the desert!
'It is not wrong to fight for justice.'

On funeral day the banner climbed and climbed with the ascending
volume till it was finally pitched on the highest mine dump in the
Rand, guarded by three gifts from friends: a tank, a rocket and a gun.

When recognition finally came with the eye of the sun, when
reckoning itemised the score, as it always must, 'Soweto' was sowing
the fallen seeds in NANCEFIELD or NICEFIELD depending on who might
be inclined to pronounce a fertile cemetery created by the marriage of
law and order to dead labour. Also, NICEFEEL underlines the peculi-
arities of the tongue contorted into foreignness as respect hovered over
the only space left in Johannesburg where police did not demand a
pass. Isn't it the only land Africans possess citizenship after death?

But seeds are bound to germinate. For funeral day, the seeds were
now bound to the mother of us all and underground they had privileged
rights to spread wide, widely extending themselves and prospering in
the eternity of creation. Ī oadcast. And if one reaps what one sows, in
a land, where the latter is black and the former white, they all worked
for fields and feels of sumptuous bullets, banquets of blasting rights of
privilege. At the moment of benediction, from grave to grave of soil-
streaming mounds with her, mount Freedom banner.

As each shovel blanketed our reservoirs of tears and grief, the little
girl followed the ministerial 'dust unto dust' with verses from class
recitation:

> it is ours
> this land
> the air
> the water and sun
> it is ours
>
> when someone says nay nay nay
> say I beg your pardon, nay.
>
> also ours the mountains
> the fruits in valleys
> from end to endless end
> ours all

the breath in live blades
the pulse of our wind
altogether ours

when some say mine mine mine
say I beg, beg your pardon,
nay ours ours
remember our sweat
too is ours
dead people's sweat
we will not forget
when we still bleed
our pain also pours
ours the scattered grains
to cement
to build
and to build over.

Amen. Five times – differing melodies,
the last deep in the throat and the chest – husky,
positive.

Amen? Johannesburg is the child of 'Soweto'. Aah! Amen Stranger!

Don't be alarmed at such an umbilical existence. The reverse of the question would be more appropriate to answer but since a child of 'Soweto' significantly differs from a Johannesburg darling we shall again ask the question direct: Where is Johannesburg without 'Soweto'? If the cemetery suggests itself, blame it on the gold deposited below the earth we trample.

Without Johannesburg, Soweto lives and dies. Dies as South Western Township, dies as dependence and gold. Lives as full humanity, peoplehood! Ours.

•

Amen. So be it.
This will be.

DANIEL MANDISHONA

A wasted land

Uncle Nicholas came back from England after the war in January 1981. He spent the entire fourteen hours that the journey lasted trussed up in a straitjacket between two burly cabin crew. On arrival at the airport he was met by a four-car police escort and taken straight to the psychiatric unit at Harare Hospital. For his waiting relatives, most of whom had not seen him for twenty-five years, it was a traumatic homecoming.

I had been born in his absence and only knew him from a sepia-edged black and white photograph which he had sent to my father on his arrival. It was of him and a friend standing ankle-deep in fresh snow with pigeons perched on their heads and arms. Throughout most of my childhood my memory of him consisted of that hazy, unsatisfactory likeness that was twenty years out of date. Yet it told me nothing about his behavioural quirks: how he talked, how he walked, how he laughed; whether he drank or smoked. In short, I could not visualise the whole without knowing its parts.

When he killed himself in March 1982 by cutting his wrists, all I was left with were confused memories of weekly visits to the hospital bed of a druggy and pathetic old man, who soiled himself and had to be chained to the bed posts to curtail the intermittent orgies of self-inflicted violence provoked by deep bouts of melancholy. It was an inescapable yet poignant irony that he had gone overseas to better himself, not to come back in disgrace to swell the ranks of burned-out, unhinged 'been-tos' with minds contaminated by too much learning.

For the last eight years of his exile he had stopped writing altogether. My father wrote to him regularly but in the end stopped because all his letters were returned saying there was no such person known at that address. Nobody knew what Uncle Nicholas was doing or where he was doing it. Eventually, it seemed, nobody cared much. We knew he was still alive because he sent the occasional Christmas card, and sometimes we went to the post office to collect boxes of second-hand clothes he bought at street markets. When my paternal grandmother died he did not know about it until my father sent a message with a woman who had won a British Council scholarship to study pharmacy at the same college that was Uncle Nicholas's last known abode.

Up to this day nobody knows why he went mad, or why in the end he thought it necessary to take his own life. His madness gradually got worse and in the end, out of sheer desperation, Father had to take him out of the hospital and put him into the care of a traditional witchdoctor. At night he hardly slept, consumed as he was by terrifying nightmares in which he was pursued by the demons that had taken up residence in his unhinged mind and so corrupted his language that all he was capable of was a dialect of carnal profanities. He slept a lot, ate very little and soon managed to reduce himself to a gaunt mass of bones.

The witchdoctor left one rainy night and never came back.

●

Later on we were to learn – through unsubstantiated rumour, naturally – that after completing his studies he had moved on to Manchester, taken an English wife, and fathered several children. The story was all the more incredible because in Rhodesia he was still married to my Aunt Emily, with whom he had three grown-up children. Another rumour, from a different source, said he had subsequently spent six years in a British jail for wife-battery and child-abuse. This seemed to explain his long silence in the middle of the 70s. When he came out his wife had the marriage annulled on the grounds of his cruelty. She sought a court order that prevented him from seeing his own children. He foolishly threatened to kill her and got himself deported. Those who had nothing better to do than speculate about the reasons for his madness identified the woman's callousness as the pebble that dislodged the avalanche of derangement that finally overwhelmed him.

Sometimes I would look at that old black and white photograph, which my father had relegated from pride of place in the living room to the back of his bedroom door, and wonder how such a brilliant and gifted man could have been capable of the cruelties that were alleged of him. Yet it is quite often said that the calmest features hide the most scheming minds. In the early years my father made sure that everybody in the street and beyond knew that his 'kid brother' Nicholas Musoni – the precociously gifted former herd-boy who wrote prize-winning essays on the Pioneer Column and the Great Trek and the Battle of Blood River – was studying clinical pharmacology at the University of London; that when he completed his doctorate he would be the first indigenous black Rhodesian to hold such a qualification. On most occasions the boast was met by politely bemused blank stares: Pharmacology? – was it something to do with farming, perhaps . . . ? Father's simplified explanation was to tell people that Uncle Nicholas was learning how to make Cafenol and Disprin.

Yes, Uncle Nicholas, even though he might not have not known it himself, was a man on the verge of creating momentous history.

But in the days after Uncle Nicholas's death and before his own suicide my father rarely talked about him. When he did he no longer referred to him as 'my kid brother' but as 'that unfortunate brother of mine'. It was almost as if he felt that by propagating this subtle but unbrotherly denunciation he could distance himself from the accusatory fingers that were looking for somewhere to point. He after all had been the instigator of Uncle Nicholas's decision to study abroad. In truth, there had been nowhere for him to go after he had been expelled from the University of Rhodesia for his political activities. The letters he wrote in his first year abroad were all opened by the Special Branch before they were delivered, usually a good month from the date of the postmark. Once, we even got a Christmas card from him a week before Easter.

Despite the fact that he was thousands of miles away in England, Uncle Nicholas was as much a victim of the war as us who were right there in the middle of the bloody conflict. Wars claim their victims in many different ways. They have tentacles that reach beyond the definable violence of battlefields and muddy trenches. They continue to claim casualties long after the physical wounds of shrapnel and gunfire have healed. There is no doubt in my mind that the enforced exile that alienated Uncle Nicholas played a crucial part in his illness.

As the doctors at the hospital told Father the day they discharged him, there was nothing physically wrong with him. Whatever he had was all in his head. He was much too young when he left for London. Too young and too inexperienced to cope with the exhilarating freedoms of his new world; a world that was so different from the one he had left behind.

•

I was ten when the war started and twenty-one when it ended. In between I lost most of my youth and some of my best friends. Ishmael, Garikayi, Kingston, Jabulani, Abednigo. These were people I had known since childhood without realising that they harboured grudges far deeper than mine. When they were all killed on the same night trying to cross the Mozambique/Rhodesia border I felt cheated and angry because they had left me out of their doomed plan. And yet I also knew that had they invited me to join I would have found a reason for not going. I was simply not strong enough, or perhaps I was just a coward.

The first time I realised there was a war on was when some of Father's people came down from the villages and vowed never to return. Before that I had always thought of the war as something that happened to other people – like freak accidents, natural disasters and fatal diseases. These people from operational area villages spoke of landmines and dusk-to-dawn curfews; of the mangled corpses of civilians 'caught in cross-fire' and of road blocks manned by sadistic soldiers; of stealthy midnight air-raids that dropped bombs that peeled off skin and burnt the flesh to the bone. Raids that flattened whole villages and filled orphanages with children who would grow up without ever knowing who their parents were or what they looked like.

The country was a wasteland of pain and heartache. Events were happening much too fast for them to be seen as anything other than an incoherent jumble of random circumstances that rolled headlong into each other, cartwheeling towards even worse disasters. The conflict became an indecisive tussle of divergent wills; of peripheral battles vying to influence an outcome that was already decided.

The violence was the worst part.

It so bludgeoned our senses that in the end we became immune to it, like a tired horse that can no longer respond to the stinging pain of the jockey's whip. Each passing day I watched my mother grow old with the violence; embittered, disconsolate, unforgiving. For it was a violence that encapsulated in its obscene wholeness the disarray that military confrontation breeds. The nationalist politicians indulged in ritualised displays of reciprocal insults that only served as a tool for the unsympathetic press to explore the dark depths of their ignorance. They waved militant placards and when on television droned on and on and on like demented sleep-talkers. They proclaimed a fragile unity yet the only thing they had in common, like travellers on the same road, was the destination – not the means of getting there nor the best course to take.

They were an assortment of vainglorious misfits stultified by a communal dearth of intellect. They were men of many promises but few deeds, each pulling in his own direction, each vying to impose his own will. Their speeches were long on emotion and rhetoric but short on ideas. They talked unrealistically of dismantling by proletarian revolution a political system that had been in place for over a century. A political order that was so deeply rooted in the very fabric of the society it had created that it could only be destroyed at considerable expense to the society itself.

The nationalist politicians and the government were like a parasite and its host animal who need each other because of the mutual benefit of an otherwise harmful co-existence. They talked and talked and got nowhere. We listened to both of them, hoping some day they would remove their blinkers and start to make sense. We could see that their promised land would be a tainted utopia, a paradise of emptiness. Yet somehow we listened to them and followed them like columns of compliant somnambulists to the edge of the chasm. Perhaps we were naive to do so, but the situation dictated a response fashioned not by reason but by impulse: the impulse of survival. After the war the same people were to swiftly change sides and stand on rostrums and claim credit for a victory that everybody knew was not theirs.

It is truly amazing how expediency can make people have different memories of the same thing.

•

I remember going to the funerals of relatives who broke one curfew too many and ended up riddled with bullets in dusty roadside ditches.

We lived in Bindura at the time. It was an old colonial house; so old that sometimes when it rained the walls shook and the windows rattled and the zinc roof produced the most astounding din. Each night we arranged cups and saucers and buckets on the floor to catch the new leaks. We spent many Christmases huddled by the fire in the front room, roasting peanuts and mice to while away the tedium of long slow nights. By staying up late and waking early we sustained the illusion that the days were long and the nights short. Our mother told us stories of her own childhood, growing up in a country that would perhaps be irrevocably lost to us. When we went to bed we pressed our ears hard against the walls and listened to the thunder-roll of gun-battles raging in valleys full of ghost towns long deserted by all sane people. In the long silences that followed sporadic lulls in hostilities our lives were full of fear and uncertainty. Yet even the silence had its own smells; its own ghostly cadences that hung to every long moment.

We celebrated New Year's Eve wondering how many of us would make it through the horrors of the next twelve months. We watched army helicopters gliding like sinister dragonflies on daily manoeuvres to flush out the unseen enemy, rotors swirling in the haze, flattening the grass. Our race-fixated masters had us by the scruff of the neck and they would not let go. Having shut the outside world out – and us in – they were, like caged animals in a zoo, the undisputed masters of their insular kingdom.

Even before Uncle Nicholas's death, we all knew that Father's businesses weren't doing too well. We knew he couldn't get supplies for the two grocery shops that provided our livelihood. The truck drivers, understandably, had reservations about driving along roads that took them through the treacherous terrain of the war zone. There was a fortnightly army convoy that came our way but the supplies, when they arrived, ran out in three or four days. The few drivers who dared drive through the operational areas at night demanded exorbitant payments of 'danger money'. After all, they said, they were risking life and limb.

It did not matter that they were on the same side as the guerillas. Landmines and bazookas were colour-blind.

He was a proud man, my father. Perhaps it was this unfortunate tribal trait that fostered within his stubborn head a self-deluding and dangerous overestimation of his own capabilities. He soon found himself, indefatigable optimist that he was, marooned alone in a sea of chronic pessimism. Beleaguered and yet stoically heroic, he dealt with the considerable strain of his fluctuating fortunes by calmly playing down his many failures and exaggerating the few successes. My mother worried constantly about him, for she had known him far too long to be fooled by the elaborate masquerade of normality with which he sought to hide his quite substantial anxieties.

Yet within his bounteous heart he harboured humanitarian sympathies that went beyond the call of duty. People came down from the villages and he was sufficiently moved by their plight to unselfishly borrow money and help them start new lives away from the incessant boom of guns and mortar shells. But in the end he became a victim of his own exemplary altruism. People simply took advantage of him.

When the war intensified the supplies stopped altogether. A convoy was ambushed near Devil's Hill and fifteen Rhodesian army soldiers killed. So our side was winning the war, but at what cost? The shops had row upon row of empty shelves as business slackened considerably. There was no bread, sugar, eggs, soap, salt, milk, butter. In fact, there was nothing. Disgruntled regulars took their custom elsewhere. The point was soon reached where the monthly lease repayments on the buildings far exceeded the profits the businesses themselves were making. The three girls Father employed, distant cousins brought in as a favour after special pleading from their parents who were worried that continued unemployment might lead them into premature motherhood, were now threatening to take their erstwhile benefactor to court for non-payment of wages. They appreciated their employer's plight but insisted that their own difficulties were now just as pressing.

One afternoon an unmarked van from Zimbabwe Furnitures arrived to cart away our threadbare living room suite. Mother told prying neighbours that it was going back to be reupholstered. She too had started telling little lies to maintain the family's good name. That night she sat alone by the fire and cried herself to sleep. We sold things in the house so Father could pay off his debts. He said his insolvency was a temporary hiccup; a minor occupational blip he would soon overcome. But by then I think even he knew that he was fooling no one. He had to borrow money off one loan shark to pay off another. It became an endless spiral of debt. Sometimes he spent hours in the shops and came back bleary-eyed and pensive. He was a broken man.

I hated the war for what it was doing to him, and what it was making him do to us.

●

On the day of Uncle Nicholas's funeral Father had to go to court again. One of his unpaid creditors had run out of patience and sympathy and issued a writ. The funeral itself was delayed because of heavy seasonal rain. They put the coffin in the living room with its top open and the body garlanded by flowers. There was a heavy, overpowering scent in the air. I went in alone and stared at Uncle Nicholas's dead mad face. It was smooth, like a chiselled slab of pasty grey skin. The facial muscles had been frozen into a rigid, lopsided snarl that gave his normally pious features the appearance of a petrified gargoyle. His hands were clasped across his chest as if in prayer, the cuffs of his favourite shirt judiciously covering the wrists he had slashed with the bread knife.

His eldest daughter, Michelle, had arrived unannounced from Manchester the previous day for the funeral. She exhausted herself being friendly to the point of sycophancy with everybody she spoke to but it was all in vain. Aunt Emily, Uncle Nicholas's widow, had made sure that the girl would feel unwelcome by shamelessly orchestrating a verbal boycott directed at her and her white boyfriend. Most of the people Michelle spoke to spoke back in Shona even though they knew fully well that she was a stranger to both the country and its language. I felt sorry for her, yet at the same time I was also ashamed at allowing myself to be party to such a disgraceful conspiracy. But Aunt Emily had made it known, quite emphatically, that she held the girl's mother solely responsible for my uncle's fatal madness. It was an unfair charge but Aunt Emily had always been inclined towards mindless vindictiveness.

Outside the house women in black veils stood patiently on the deep veranda. Some sang hymns, others chatted about the continuing drought. The men held subdued conversations that centred on the estate of the departed man. By mid-afternoon Father had still not returned. The rain by that time had stopped. A straggly rainbow appeared on the edge of the sky but its colours were not quite right; they were frayed and indistinct. My left eye had an autonomous twitch that portended unfavourable news. The rain stopped an hour later and the hearse arrived to lead the procession to the cemetery.

My father had still not returned.

•

Bernard . . . Run to the shop, said my mother, and phone the court to see what has happened to your father. We cannot bury his brother without him there . . .

•

I took the shop keys and dashed off to the smaller of the two grocery shops. There was a telephone in a back office which Father used to ring up the Mount Darwin Indian wholesalers who supplied most of his stock. And that was where I found him, slumped across the counter with his wrists cut and his shirtsleeves drenched in brilliant splashes of clotted blood. He was surrounded by unpaid invoices and court summonses. He had been drinking heavily. Several bottles of Bols brandy were on the floor. The Chinese doctor who came from Bindura Hospital said he had been dead for four or five hours at least. There was a bottle of rat poison by his side, long opened but still emitting a faint pungent odour. He had drunk that too. Your father must have really wanted to die, said the doctor, making his astute observation sound as if it was a compliment.

The time of death coincided with the time he had left the house. I knew then that he had never intended to go to the court. That evening I went back to the shop and removed all the court summonses I could find from the office and burnt them in the backyard. I did not think it either fair or necessary for my mother's heartbreak to be compounded by the revelation that our comfortable lifestyle had been fraudulently financed.

●

The judge declared him a bankrupt in his absence and ordered sequestration of all movable assets. All the court cases against him were dropped because there was nobody to prosecute. Bailiffs arrived over the next few days to apportion the remaining things in the shops and the house to pay off his creditors. They literally left us in the clothes we were standing in. Mother had to borrow money from relatives to pay for the funeral. Michelle came to tell us that she had booked into a cheaper motel and would be staying for the second funeral. Mother was so touched by this gesture that she dropped her pretended hostility and even invited Michelle and her boyfriend to a meal. But they never came. When I went to their motel I was told they had left urgently. I wrote her a letter, speculatively using one of Uncle Nicholas's old addresses, but it came back saying there was no such person known at that address.

●

We moved house after that but we could not erase the memory of Father's death. One cannot rid a room of its bad associations by rearranging the furniture. Father died in April 1981, exactly a year after Independence. Those debts accumulated during the war proved too much even for a man of his resilience. Like Uncle Nicholas and so many others, he survived the war only to die of its effects when the peace arrived.

MIA COUTO

The birds of God

Begging your pardon, I don't know anything more like a pilgrim than the river. The waves pass by on a journey which has no end. For how long has it been water's job to do that? Alone in his old dugout, Ernesto Timba measured his life. At the age of twelve he had entered the school of pulling fish from the water. Ever in the waft of the current, his shadow had reflected the laws of the river dweller for the last thirty years. And what was it all for? Drought had exhausted the earth, the seeds were not fulfilling their promise. When he returned from fishing, he had nothing to defend himself from his wife and children, who impaled him with their eyes. Eyes like those of a dog, he was loath to admit, but the truth is that hunger makes men like animals.

While he contemplated his suffering, Timba made his craft glide slowly along. Under the *mafurreira* tree, there on the bank where the river narrows, he brought the boat to rest so that he might drive away his sad thoughts. He allowed his paddle to nibble the water and the dugout clung to the stillness. But he could not stop his thoughts:

'*What life have I lived? Water, water, just nothing else.*'

As it rocked to and fro, the dugout caused his anguish to multiply.

'*One day they'll fish me out of the water, swallowed up by the river.*'

He foresaw his wife and children watching him being pulled from the mud, and it was as if the roots of the water were being torn up.

Overhead, the *mafurreira* retained the sun's fierce dispatch. But Timba wasn't listening to the tree, his eyes were peeping into his soul. And it was as if they were blind, for pain is a dust which drains light away. Still higher above, morning called and he caught the smell of the intense blue.

'*If only I belonged to the sky,*' he sighed.

And he felt the burden of thirty years of tiredness upon his life. He remembered the words of his father, uttered to teach him courage:

'*See the hunter there, what he does? He prepares his spear the moment he sees the gazelle. But the fisherman can't see the fish inside the river. The fisherman believes in something he can't see.*'

That was the lesson of the bound-to-be of life and he now recalled those wise words. It was getting late and hunger told him it was time to go home. He began to move his arm while casting a last glance upwards, beyond the clouds. It was then that a huge bird passed over the sky. It was like a king, pleased with its own majesty. The creature, high on the wing, held his eyes and an uncanny anxiety took root within him. He thought:

'*If that bird were to fall on my canoe now!*'

He uttered these words aloud. Hardly had he finished speaking than the bird shook its huge wings and quickly flew in a downward spiral towards the boat. It fell as if expelled from life. Timba picked up the damaged bird and holding it in his hands, saw that the blood had not yet unbuttoned its body. In the boat, the animal gradually recovered, until it stood up and climbed onto the prow to take stock of its survival. Timba grabbed it, and weighed its flesh in order to work out how many meals it would provide. He put the idea out of his mind, and with a shove, helped the bird to take off.

'*Be off with you, bird, go back from where you came!*'

But the bird turned round and headed back to the boat. The fisherman once again drove it away. Yet again it returned. Ernesto Timba began to despair.

'*Get back to your life, you bloody bird.*'

Nothing. The bird didn't move. It was then that the fisherman began to wonder: that thing wasn't a bird, it was a sign from God. The warning from heaven would destroy his peace of mind for ever.

Accompanied by the animal, he returned to the village. His wife celebrated his homecoming:

'*Let's have the bird for lunch!*'

Delighted, she called the children:

'*Little ones, come and see the dicky-bird.*'

Without answering, Timba placed the bird on the mat and went to the back of the house to fetch some wooden boards, wire and reeds.

Then he set to work to build a cage so large that even a man could fit inside standing up straight. He put the animal inside and fed it the fish he had caught.

His wife was flabbergasted: the man was mad. Time passed and Timba only cared about the bird.

His wife would ask, pointing at the bird:

'*Seeing as how hunger is pinching us, don't you want to kill it?*'

Timba would raise his arm, emphatically. '*Never! Whoever touched the bird would be punished by God, would be marked down for life.*'

And so the days passed by, while the fisherman awaited fresh signs of divine intentions. Countless times he lingered in the moist afternoon heat while the river sat there in front of him. When the sun went down, he would go and check the cage where the animal was growing ever fatter. Little by little, he began to notice a shadow of sadness fall over the sacred bird. He realised the creature was suffering because it was lonely. One night he asked God to send the solitary fowl a companion. The following day, the cage had a new inmate, a female. Timba silently thanked the heavens for this new gift. At the same time, anxiety took root in him: why had God entrusted him to keep these animals? What might be the message they brought?

He thought and thought. That sign, that lightning flash of white plumage, could only mean that heaven's humour was about to change. If men would agree to dispense their kindness to those messengers from heaven, then the drought would end and the season of rains would begin. It had befallen him, a poor fisherman of the river, to play host to God's envoys. It was his task to show that men could still be good. Yes, that true goodness cannot be measured in times of abundance but when hunger dances in the bodies of men.

His wife, who had returned from the *machamba*, interrupted his thoughts:

'*So there are two of them now, are there?*'

She came over, sat down on the same mat and looking long and hard into her companion's eyes, said:

'*Husband, the pot's on the fire. I'm asking you for the neck of one of them, just one.*'

It was a waste of time. Timba promised severe punishment to whoever mistreated the divine birds.

In time, the couple had chicks. There were three of them, clumsy and ugly, their gullets ever open: enough appetite to empty the river. Timba toiled on behalf of their parents. The household provisions, already so scarce, were diverted to feed the coop.

In the village, the rumour went around: Ernesto Timba was stark raving mad. His own wife, after many a threat, left home taking with her all the children. Timba didn't even seem to notice his family's absence. He was more concerned with ensuring his poultry's protection. He detected a spirit of envy around him, vengeance hatching itself. Was it his fault that he had been chosen? They said he had gone crazy. But he who is chosen by God always wanders off his path.

Then, one afternoon when he had finished his work on the river, a feeling of uncertainty set his mind aflame: the birds! He set off home at a rush. When he got near, he saw a pall of smoke rising through the trees around his house. He paddled his dugout towards the river bank, jumped out without even tying it up, and began to run towards the scene of the tragedy. When he arrived, all he saw was wreckage and ashes. The wood and wire had been chewed up by the flames. From between the boards a wing, untouched by the fire, sought to save itself. The bird must have hurled itself against the wall of flames and the wing had got away, an arrow ominously pointing towards disaster. It was not swaying to and fro, as is the obsession of dead things. It was rigid, full of certainty.

Timba stepped back, appalled. He shouted for his wife, for his children, and then, on discovering that there was nobody else to shout for, he wept such copious tears of rage that his eyes hurt.

Why? Why had they harmed those birds, pretty as they were? And there and then, amidst all the ash and the smoke, he addressed himself to God:

'*You're going to be angry, I know. You're going to punish your children. But look: I'm asking you to forgive them. Let me be the one to die, me. Leave the others to suffer what they are already suffering. You can forget the rain even, you can leave the dust lying on the ground, but please don't punish the men of this land.*'

The following day, they found Ernesto hugging the current of the river, chilled by the early morning mist. When they tried to raise him, they found him heavy and impossible to separate from the water. The strongest men were brought to the task, but their efforts were in vain.

The body was stuck to the surface of the river. A strange feeling of dread spread among those present. To hide their fear, someone said:

'*Go and tell his wife. Tell the others that the village madman has died.*'

And they withdrew. As they were climbing the bank, the clouds clashed, the sky seemed to cough sullenly as if it were sick. In different circumstances, they would have celebrated the coming of the rain. Not now. For the first time, their faiths joined together pleading that it might not rain.

Impassive, the river flowed on into the distance, laughing at the ignorance of men. Ernesto Timba, gently lulled by the current, was carried downstream, and shown the by-ways he had only glimpsed in dreams.

STEVE CHIMOMBO

The rubbish dump

The boy squatted on the ground, bending over a small toy car. The bodywork consisted of rectangular pieces of cardboard inserted between a forest of bent pieces of wire. The wheels were empty boot-polish tins and the steering rod was one long reed which culminated in a wheel from the top of a large baby-powder tin.

The expression on the boy's face was a study in concentration: contracted mouth, wrinkled nose, furrowed brow and slit eyes. His hands worked impatiently on short pieces of wire that had come loose in the chassis. After a moment, he straightened up with a satisfied grunt, revved the engine, and burst into song:

> *Azungu nzeru*
> *kupanga ndege*
> *si kanthu kena*
> *koma ndi khama.*

The shrill notes pierced the air and filled the civil service quarters for a few minutes. The song was interrupted by the squeak, rattle and thump of a wheelbarrow along the dusty road twenty yards away from the last row of houses. The boy's song dangled in the air, faltered, and fell. The squeak, rattle and thump increased steadily in volume as it approached.

It was Mazambezi. That's what everyone called him – behind his back. Mazambezi, the airport garbage collector, pushing his wheelbarrow.

The boy stopped manoeuvring the car into the space between the two broken bricks. His body went slack as he remembered that it was Friday and he had missed the big plane landing, coming from London. Locally, they called it 'Four Engine'. Mazambezi was bringing in the rubbish from that plane, which meant it had landed hours ago. The

boy cursed himself for having forgotten to be on the balcony to wa
the passengers in their expensive clothes stepping down from the plane,
carrying large bags, cameras and all sorts of mysterious things from
far-off lands. It was now too late to run to the airport. The visitors
would have been driven off to their various destinations by now. Even
the outgoing passengers would have boarded the plane.

The increasingly piercing whine of a plane about to take off
confirmed this. The boy gazed at where he knew the plane would
appear in the sky. A moment later, the corrugated-iron rooftops rattled
violently as the thundering roar threatened to tear them off. This was
one disadvantage of living near an international airport. Every now
and then, the staff quarters were shattered by mini-earthquakes caused
by planes landing or taking off. Not that the boy minded. The noise
filled him with an almost superstitious awe and reverence at the
intelligence that could make those big things fly like that in the sky.

A few minutes later, the boy was straining his eyes to follow the
silver streak overtaking and outstripping the clouds. After a moment or
two, he could see it no longer. He wondered who would be on it today,
and where they would be going. His father had once told him that the
plane stopped at such places as Salisbury and Johannesburg, before
going on to England. When he could read, he would have fun finding
these places in the book his father had told him all the famous places
on earth were written. Still, it was a pity he had not been on the
balcony today.

The rumble of the wheelbarrow was very near now. It sounded like
the feeble spluttering of an ancient motorcycle, too old to start yet
persisting in igniting for a few moments. The boy manoeuvred his car
between the two bricks and took the path that joined the road
Mazambezi would take. The rubbish dump was only a hundred yards
away from his house.

'*Moni*, Joey,' the man greeted the boy.

'*Moni*.' Joey stopped a few feet away to watch his progress.

'You haven't gone to school today?'

'We've got a month's holiday.'

'That's good.'

'What have you got this time?'

'I don't know,' Mazambezi replied. 'A few pieces of cheese mixed with vomit, maybe.'

Joey crinkled his nose at the mention of vomit. Someone had told him once that the passengers on the plane sometimes vomited in bags provided for that purpose. Joey wondered what made people vomit when flying in a plane. He had seen his father vomit in the house when drunk. It was not very nice.

Joey kept his distance and watched the old man push the antiquated machine in front of him. The machine seemed to be an extension of Mazambezi. Joey could not imagine him without it, nor it without him. Both had been one of the first quaint scenes he had noticed when his family had been transferred to this airport district.

The machine had once been a gleaming piece of metal like the shiny planes at the airport, but that must have been long ago, in the hardware shop. Now it was marked at irregular rusty intervals with layers of flattened, dried-out bits of what once had been cheese, canned beef and other such nondescript things. It wore the indifferent colour of a piece of metal dug up from damp earth after ages. The wheel revolved round a worn-out axle. This was where the agonising squeak came from. Apparently grease had been applied to stop it, but that too was years ago. Only blackened encrustations were left to commemorate the fact.

They made quite a pair, these two: the dry and wet seasons had left their marks on both man and machine. The tattered rags of the old man were more suitable for the pit than for wearing. Clearly visible in many places through the torn overalls were multi-coloured – because of additional patches – khaki shorts. An equally ancient army jungle hat, pulled closely over the head, served as protection against the dry heat. The brim had a wide gash in it, so that the headgear was more of a cap than anything else. The short black hair underneath was mixed with a lot of grey, giving it the colour of sooty lime.

The rubbish pit made itself felt as they neared. Wave after wave of stench enveloped Joey and Mazambezi, and went on in its oppressive embrace to the native quarters.

Joey remembered the revulsion he had felt during the first days he had noticed Mazambezi's daily ritual. He had followed the old man after a week or two of suppressed curiosity. Joey had wondered what made the old man take so long at the rubbish pit after tipping his load. The odour had got thicker and more oppressive as he had crept nearer and nearer where the old man sat gazing into the pit. Joey's nostrils twitched violently as the offensive rush of foul air flowed into him, past him, until he felt as though he was swimming in liquid rot. It clawed at his throat and settled in his stomach. Nausea hit him. He stumbled over a projection and cried out as he fell on to some disgustingly soft, sticky substance. He shuddered at the contact, convulsed for a few moments, and retched painfully. A hand fell on his shoulder as he tried to get to his feet.

'Are you all right?' The gruff voice of the old man seemed to come out of the ooze around him.

'Don't touch me!' he shouted. His face contorted, he sprawled backwards into the mess again, instinctively recoiling from the other.

'I said, are you all right?'

'Don't come near me!' he yelled wrathfully. 'You dirty, filthy, old Mazambezi!'

The old man straightened up slowly. Joey succeeded in his second attempt to get up, and sped off across the field that separated the pit from the houses. He glanced back once, from a safe distance, to see the old man settle back in the position he had found him in. Well, Joey thought, at least he had satisfied his curiosity. The old man spent some time rummaging in the debris and salvaged left-over food from the load. This he piled on to a piece of paper and ate. In his blindness, Joey had fallen trying to communicate to the man in the tower at the airport in Tokyo, in the manner his father had taught him: 'Request permission to land,' he intoned over and over again as he circled round, 'request permission to land. Can you hear me? Over.'

'Look, Joey,' a voice interrupted the pilot. 'I've got a real plane for you.'

It was Mazambezi. He had walked soundlessly from the pit without his wheelbarrow, and was holding out a miniature 'Air Rhodesia' to him. Joey looked fearfully at him. The brown eyes were almost apologetic. The boy backed a step, his mouth working. He glanced at his home, grabbed the plane, and ran as fast as he could to behind the kitchen. There he knelt down and held the plane to his chest, and panted for a few minutes. There were tears in his eyes as, after a time, he looked again about him. The old man was gone. Joey had not heard the wheelbarrow grinding off. He stood up and peeked round the corner of the kitchen. He pulled back and put the plane under his shirt. It made a bulge that would not have deceived anyone. Joey quickly crossed his arms where the bulges were most pronounced. With a palpitating heart, he started shaking his shoulders ostentatiously, all the while walking towards the house singing:

> *Azungu nzeru*
> *kupanga ndege*
> *si kanthu kena*
> *koma ndi khama.*

Luckily, his mother was cleaning the main bedroom. Joey ran to the little room where he slept. He found his school bag with some exercise books in it and quickly hid his 'Air Rhodesia' in there. Among the school books were an odd assortment of foreign coins, tourist guides, empty cigarette packets and so on, collected from the airport. Every time he went to the balcony, he came back with one or two more items to add to his treasure. During the holidays, it was easy to hide them there. No one would think of looking for anything in his bag.

Joey unrolled his sleeping mat and lay down. He listened to his mother cleaning. His arm stole to the bag and came out with the plane. He inspected it carefully. It had a broken tail, but if he held it where the tail should have been it would pass as an airworthy craft.

'Joey! Are you in there?'

'Yes, Mother,' Joey answered, precipitately shoving the plane back into the bag and pushing it against the wall. When the door opened, he was breathing heavily on the mat.

'What are you doing down there?' His mother's imposing frame filled the doorway.

'I – I have a headache, Mother.'

'Why didn't you tell me?'

'You were busy, Mother.'

'Too busy to tell me you are ill?'

'I – I –'

'Come here, Joey.'

'Yes, Mother.'

'Now, I won't have you pretending you're sick.' The inevitable finger was two inches away from his nose.

'No, Mother.'

'I saw you running about and singing not a few minutes ago.'

'I – I – Mother – '

'Don't lie to me.'

'No, Mother.'

'Good. Now, I want you to go to the grocery to get me a pound of sugar and a packet of tea leaves.'

'Yes, Mother.'

'Here's the money.'

Joey took the money without a word and went out, worried. What if his mother found the plane? He sped to the grocery and was back in record time. His mother met him with, 'I thought you had a terrible headache.'

'I – I – it's gone, Mother.'

'Good. Now, help me move these things so that I can clean your room. Do you have to be so messy?'

Joey ran to the school bag and held it tightly against him.

'I said everything, not just your bag.'

'Yes, Mother.'

Joey put the bag gingerly on top of his other books, clothes and mat, and carried them out of the room. He put them in a corner and stood over them. Moments later, his mother called out to him that she had finished. Another careful operation took the objects back to his room.

'You're acting very strangely.' His mother was looking hard at him. 'Are you sure your headache is gone?'

'No, Mother.' Joey avoided looking at his mother. 'It's come back.'

'Maybe,' she said. 'You can lie down.'

Joey unrolled his mat again and lay down. He felt calmer now. His father came home late that night, drunk again and singing, 'For he's a jolly good fellow, and so say all of *me*.' Joey listened as he noisily asked for his supper. His mother's voice came faintly to Joey's ears at intervals, as his father explained loudly that a white man had bought him the drinks. The white man was a nice man, he proclaimed, for – it was his favourite question – where would the black man be without him? When he was in that mood, he could be tedious. He would go on enumerating the good things the white man had brought to the country: jobs, cars, aeroplanes, not to mention booze. Joey fell asleep as the voice droned on about Africans, who should be eternally grateful, now living in decent houses, wearing decent clothes, and leading decent lives. His mother had retired to the bedroom, although he knew she was listening. His father spoke for all the world to hear.

It took Joey a week to muster enough courage to go and meet Mazambezi on the road. He thanked him shyly for the plane, but the old man only grunted something that was drowned in the squeak, rattle, thump of the wheelbarrow. Joey followed hesitantly behind the two. The old man's cracked feet made little eddies of dust as he trudged on. The overalls were as soiled as the machine. Joey quickened his steps to walk alongside Mazambezi.

'What have you got this time?'

'I don't know.' The old man was looking straight ahead of him. 'A few lumps of meat with the usual mixture.'

Joey was careful not to crinkle his face. The man and the boy turned into the path that led to the rubbish dump. The nauseating smell got stronger as they got nearer.

The pit was very old and large, but shallow. It had been there long before Joey was born. The original rubbish had putrefied enough to turn into earth underneath. It was not Mazambezi alone who used the place. The civil servants also did. It abounded in greying pieces of *nsima* scraped from the bottoms of pots, yellows and greens of banana, pawpaw and orange peel, chaff of sugar cane or maize, not to mention baby, chicken and dog shit. Every imaginable kind of waste matter found its way into the pit. The fresh rubbish, the insides of chicken and guts of fish, were feasts for bloated bluebottles. They and the fruit flies buzzed angrily like bees, when the man and the boy reached the mouth of the pit. The crows circled above them, cawing noisily. Other forms of life bred in the empty milk, fish and beef cans strewn about the pit.

'Did all that come from the plane?'

'Yes.'

'They must eat a lot.'

'When the white man eats, he eats.'

'It's not only the white man who travels in the planes.'

'No. But still it's the white man's food. You don't see *khobwe* or *mgaiwa* in the wheelbarrow, do you?'

'No. What do the Wenela people eat?'

'Bread.'

'Oh?'

'Just imagine,' Mazambezi was all of a sudden talkative. He had stopped the wheelbarrow at the edge of the pit and picked out a can from its depths. 'Just imagine,' he repeated vehemently. 'Where do you think this can came from?'

'London?'

'No.'

'Paris?'

'No. It was made in Hong Kong,' he announced triumphantly. 'I sit here every day and look into the pit. I pick up bits of paper or beef cans and look at them and imagine where they came from. Japan? Russia? England? America? South Africa? As I sit here munching bits of cheese, a whole world is opened up to me. How many thousands of miles has this can of fish travelled? What places has this empty packet of biscuits visited? What person vomited into this bag? What language does he speak? What hopes and dreams does he have? I don't need to ride in their planes. As I sit here, Russia, America, Hong Kong, England are all in my grasp. They all find their way into this rubbish dump.'

'I do the same,' Joey interrupted, 'when I go to the balcony to watch the planes come and go. Every day at school, as I open my books, I wonder if I will ever be educated enough to read more about these places. Even visit them. Just imagine being able to walk in the streets of London or New York or Tokyo!'

'I know how you feel.' Mazambezi had a faraway expression on his face as he looked at the boy beside him.

'But I've also seen the places.' Joey's eyes lit up.

'Have you?'

'Yes. Every day, when I drive my car, or fly the plane you gave me, I see them so clearly. I drink Coca Cola in New York, have tea in London, and go for a drive in Tokyo.'

They sat at the edge of the dump, legs dangling into the pit, and looked at the broken bottles made in England, or squashed cans of food

made in the USA, and plastic odds and ends made in Japan or Russia.
Each was lost in his own thoughts. Humid putrefaction wafted around
them, into them, and through them to the native quarters. The crows
circled above them like black planes about to land. In the dump, the
yellow, grey and brown flies also circled and dived into juicy offal.

'Here,' the old man interrupted their dreams, 'have a piece of cheese.
Maybe it came from South Africa.'

Joey stretched out a hand. He had decided to lean against the
wheelbarrow for more comfort. He chewed the stale cheese, silently
watching the antics of the flies on a pool of vomit. The buzzing of the
flies and the cries of the crows seemed to be the only sounds, but this
was interrupted by the rising cadences of a plane starting up.

'It's the "Four Engine",' Joey remarked.

'Yes, it's the big plane taking off.'

'I wonder if it will stop in Salisbury.'

'Maybe.'

'I wonder who's in it?'

'Oh, the usual. Rich fat white men, brown men, and a few blacks.'

'Students going for more education.'

'Yes, I forgot about those.' Mazambezi stood up with a grunt, and
wiped calloused hands on his overalls. 'I've got to be going too.'

'Goodbye,' said Joey slowly. He too straightened up from the
wheelbarrow. 'We'll be meeting again tomorrow?'

'Yes.' The old man lifted the bars of the machine. In a few minutes,
the squeak, rattle and thump faded in the distance. Joey wondered who
would die first – the man or the machine. The rattle, squeak and
thump of the machine and the stoic silence of the man behind it had
the same quality as the mournful hoot of an owl. But Joey knew that
the daily exchange of 'What has the big plane brought today?' – 'Oh,
bits and pieces from the white man's land' would continue for some
time yet. The left-overs, garbage and whatever would keep finding its
way into the waiting rubbish dump; the flies and crows; Mazambezi
and Joey.

E. B. DONGALA

The man

... No, this time he won't get away! After forty-eight hours, he had
been tracked down, his itinerary was known and the village where he
was hiding identified. But how many false leads there had been! He
had been seen everywhere at once, as if he had the gift of ubiquity:
dedicated militants had apparently run him down in the heart of the
country without, however, managing to capture him: a patrol which
had been parachuted into the northern swamps claimed they had badly
wounded him, providing as their only proof traces of blood that
disappeared into a ravine; frontier guards swore they had shot him in
a canoe (which had unfortunately sunk) as he tried to escape by river:
none of these claims survived closer investigation. The already tight
police net was tightened still further, new brigades of gendarmes were
created, and the army was given *carte blanche*. Soldiers invaded the
working-class quarters of the city, breaking down the doors of houses,
sticking bayonets into mattresses filled with grass and cotton, slashing
open sacks of *foo-foo*, beating with their rifle butts anyone who didn't
answer their questions quickly enough, or quite simply cutting down
anyone who dared to protest at the violation of his home. But all these
strong-arm tactics achieved nothing, and the country was on the verge
of panic. Where could he be hiding?

It had been an almost impossible exploit, for the father-founder of
the nation, the enlightened guide and saviour of the people, the great
helmsman, the president-for-life, the commander-in-chief of the armed
forces and the beloved father of the people lived in a vast palace out of
bounds to the ordinary citizen. In any case, the circular security system
contrived by an Israeli professor with degrees in war science and
counter-terrorism was impregnable. Five hundred yards from the
palace perimeter, armed soldiers stood guard at ten-yard intervals, day

and night, and this pattern was repeated at a distance of two hundred and then one hundred yards from the perimeter. The palace itself was also surrounded by a water-filled moat of immense depth swarming with African and Indian crocodiles and caymans imported from Central America which most certainly didn't feed solely on small fry, especially during the campaigns of repression that regularly fell upon the country after every genuine or mock *coup d'état*. Behind the moat was a ditch full of black mambas and green mambas whose powerful venom killed their victims on the spot. The perimeter wall itself – an enormous sixty-foot high structure of brick and stone as imposing as the wall of the Zimbabwe ruins – bristled with watch-towers, searchlights, nails, barbed wire and broken glass; access was by two enormous doors which also served as a drawbridge and were controlled from the inside alone. Finally the palace itself, the holy of holies, where the beloved father of the people lived: one hundred and fifty rooms in which scores of huge mirrors reflected everything and everyone, multiplying and reducing them *ad infinitum*, so that visitors always felt uneasy and oppressed, aware that their least gestures were being watched. Every movement, however small, was carried like an echo from room to room, from mirror to mirror, until it reached the ultimate mirror of all, the eye of the master himself, watching over that entire universe. No one knew in which room the founder-president slept, not even the well-versed prostitutes he employed for several nights at a stretch for his highly sophisticated pleasures; even less likely to know were the unspoilt, happy little girls he enjoyed deflowering between the promulgation of two decrees from his palace of wonders. But, if the beloved-father-of-the-nation-the-supreme-and-enlightened-guide-the-commander-in-chief-of-the-armed-forces-and-beneficent-genius-of-mankind was invisible in the flesh to the majority of his subjects, he was, on the other hand, everywhere present: it was a statutory requirement that his portrait should hang in all homes. The news bulletins on the radio always began and ended with one of his stirring thoughts. The television news began, continued and finished in front of his picture, and the solitary local newspaper published in every issue at least four pages of letters in which citizens proclaimed their undying affection. Everywhere present but inaccessible. That was why the exploit was impossible.

And yet he had carried it off: he had succeeded in getting into the palace, bypassing the crocodiles, the mambas and the Praetorian guards; he had succeeded in outwitting the trap of the mirrors and had executed the father of the nation as one kills a common agitator and fomentor of coups. And then he had made the return journey, avoiding the watchtowers, the drawbridge, the green mambas, the black mambas, the crocodiles, and the Praetorian guards. And escaped! Forty-eight hours later he was still free!

... And then came the rumour, no one knew where from: he had been tracked down, his itinerary was known, and the village where he was hiding had been identified; he was surrounded. This time he wouldn't get away!

Armoured cars, jeeps, and lorries full of soldiers set off at three in the morning. The tanks didn't trouble to go round the houses in the villages through which they passed, a straight line being the shortest distance between two points: villages were left burning behind them, crops were laid waste, corpses piled up in the furrows made by their caterpillar tracks. Conquerors indeed in a defeated country, they soon reached their destination. They woke up the villagers with their rifle butts. They searched everywhere, emptied the granaries, looked in the trees and inside lofts. They didn't find the man they were looking for. The officer in command of the soldiers was furious, and his neck seemed to explode under his chinstrap:

'I know he's here, the bastard who dared to murder our dear beloved founder-president who will live for ever in the pantheon of our immortal heroes. I know the miserable wretch has a beard and is blind in one eye. If you don't tell me within ten minutes where he's hiding, I'll burn all your houses, I'll take one of you at random and have him tortured and shot!'

The ten minutes passed amid a frightened silence as deep as the silence that preceded the creation of the world. Then the officer in command of the soldiers ordered the reprisals to begin. They man-handled the villagers: some were strung up by their feet and beaten; others had red pimento rubbed into their open wounds; yet others were forced to eat fresh cow dung ... The villagers didn't denounce the hunted man. So they burned all the houses in the village, and the harvest as well, the fruits of a year's labour in a country where people rarely have enough to eat. The villagers still didn't give them the information they were seeking. In fact, the reason for their silence was quite simple: they genuinely did not know who had carried out the deed.

The man had acted alone. He had spent months making his preparations, reading, studying, planning; then he had put on a false beard and covered his left eye with a black band, like a pirate. He had found how to penetrate the impregnable palace and kill the great dictator; the way he had done it was so simple he had sworn to himself that he would never reveal it, even under torture, for it could be used again. He was nevertheless surprised to see the soldiers in his village. But had they really discovered his identity or were they just bluffing? Clearly, they didn't know who he was, standing there in front of them, among his fellow villagers who were themselves in total ignorance of what he had done. There he stood, clean-shaven and with both his eyes, waiting to see what would happen next.

The officer in charge of the soldiers, a commandant, got angrier still, confronted by his victims' silence:

'I repeat for the last time! If you do not tell me where he is hiding, this bastard one-eyed son-of-a-whore without balls who has murdered our beloved president-for-life, founder of our party and leader of the nation, I'll take one of you at random and shoot him! I'll give you five minutes!'

He looked feverishly at his quartz watch. Two minutes. One minute. Thirty seconds.

'I assure you, commandant,' the village chief pleaded, 'we don't know him and we assure you he isn't in our village.'

'Too bad for you. I'm going to take a man at random and shoot him in front of you all. That will perhaps help you to understand. You, there!'

The commandant was pointing at him. He wasn't even surprised, as if he had always expected it. Deep down, it was what he wanted, for he doubted that he would be able to go through the rest of his life with an easy conscience if he allowed someone else to die in his place. He was pleased, for he would have the satisfaction of dying with his secret.

'You will be the innocent hostage who has to be sacrificed because of the obstinacy of your chief and your fellow villagers. Tie him to a tree and shoot him!'

They kicked him and beat him with rifle butts, they slashed him with bayonets. He was dragged along the ground and tied to a mango tree. His wife flung herself on him, to be brutally pulled away. Four soldiers took aim.

'One last time, tell us where the murderer is hiding.'

'I don't know, commandant!' pleaded the chief.

'Fire!'

His chest jerked forward slightly, then he collapsed without a sound. They would never find him now!

The smoke cleared. The villagers remained plunged in a deep, stunned, silence, looking at the body slumped in the coarse liana ropes. The commandant, having carried out his threat, stood before them. He hesitated, not quite sure what to threaten them with now. Overcome by an inner panic, he struggled, at least to preserve the honour of his stripes.

'Well?' he asked.

At last the villagers became aware of him again.

'Well what!' roared the chief angrily. 'I told you we didn't know the man you're looking for. You didn't believe us and now you have killed one of us. What more can I say!'

The commandant could find nothing by way of reply. He rocked on his feet, uncertain what to do next, and at last called out an order to his men:

'Attention! Form up! The hunt goes on. The bastard may be hiding in the next village. There's no time to waste. Forward march!'

Then, turning to the villagers, he screamed: 'We'll find him, the son of a bastard, we'll flush him out wherever he's hiding, we'll pull off his balls and his ears, we'll pull out his nails and his eyes, we'll hang him naked in public in front of his wife, his mother and his children, and then we'll feed him to the dogs. You have my word on that.'

The jeeps and the tanks moved off and went elsewhere in search of 'the man'.

They are still looking for him. They sense his presence; somewhere he is hiding, but where? Crushed by dictatorship, the people feel their hearts beat faster when there is talk of 'the man'. Although the country is more police-ridden than ever, although it is crawling with spies, informers and hired killers, and although he has appointed as heads of security men from his own tribe entirely loyal to his cause, the new president, the second beloved father of the nation, entrusted with the task of continuing the sacred work of the father-founder, no longer dares go out. In order to frustrate the spell, he has issued a decree proclaiming himself unkillable and immortal, but still he hides away in the depths of his palace, with its labryrinth of passages and corridors, mirrors and reflections, walled up because he doesn't know when 'the man' will suddenly appear to strike him down in his turn, so that freedom, too long suppressed, may at last burst forth.

'The man', the hope of a nation and a people that says NO, and watches . . ..

Translated from the French by Clive Wake.

ABDULRAZAK GURNAH

Cages

There were times when it felt to Hamid as if he had been in the shop always, and that his life would end there. He no longer felt discomfort, nor did he hear the secret mutterings at the dead hours of night which had once emptied his heart in dread. He knew now that they came from the seasonal swamp which divided the city from the townships, and which teemed with life. The shop was in a good position, at a major crossroads from the city's suburbs. He opened it at first light when the earliest workers were shuffling by, and did not shut it again until all but the last stragglers had trailed home. He liked to say that at his station he saw all of life pass him by. At peak hours he would be on his feet all the time, talking and bantering with the customers, courting them and taking pleasure in the skill with which he handled himself and his merchandise. Later he would sink exhausted on the boxed seat which served as his till.

The girl appeared at the shop late one evening, just as he was thinking it was time to close. He had caught himself nodding twice, a dangerous trick in such desperate times. The second time he had woken up with a start, thinking a large hand was clutching his throat and lifting him off the ground. She was standing in front of him, waiting with a look of disgust in her face.

'Ghee,' she said after waiting for a long, insolent minute. 'One shilling.' As she spoke she half-turned away, as if the sight of him was irritating. A piece of cloth was wrapped round her body and tucked in under the armpits. The soft cotton clung to her, marking the outline of her graceful shape. Her shoulders were bare and glistened in the gloom. He took the bowl from her and bent down to the tin of ghee. He was filled with longing and a sudden ache. When he gave the bowl back to her, she looked vaguely at him, her eyes distant and glazed with tiredness. He saw that she was young, with a small round face and slim neck. Without a word, she turned and went back into the darkness, taking a huge stride to leap over the concrete ditch which divided the kerb from the road. Hamid watched her retreating form and wanted to cry out a warning for her to take care. How did she know that there wasn't something there in the dark? Only a feeble croak came out as he choked the impulse to call to her. He waited, half-expecting to hear her cry out but only heard the retreating slap of her sandals as she moved further into the night.

She was an attractive girl, and for some reason as he stood thinking about her and watched the hole in the night into which she had disappeared, he began to feel disgust for himself. She had been right to look at him with disdain. His body and his mouth felt stale. There was little cause to wash more than once every other day. The journey from bed to shop took a minute or so, and he never went anywhere else. What was there to wash for? His legs were misshapen from lack of proper exercise. He had spent the day in bondage, months and years had passed like that, a fool stuck in a pen all his life. He shut up the shop wearily, knowing that during the night he would indulge the squalor of his nature.

The following evening, the girl came to the shop again. Hamid was talking to one of his regular customers, a man much older than him called Mansur who lived nearby and on some evenings came to the shop to talk. He was half-blind with cataracts, and people teased him about his affliction, playing cruel tricks on him. Some of them said of Mansur that he was going blind because his eyes were full of shit. He could not keep away from boys. Hamid sometimes wondered if Mansur hung around the shop after something, after him. But perhaps it was just malice and gossip. Mansur stopped talking when the girl approached, then squinted hard as he tried to make her out in the poor light.

'Do you have shoe polish? Black?' she asked.

'Yes,' Hamid said. His voice sounded congealed, so he cleared his throat and repeated Yes. The girl smiled.

'Welcome, my love. How are you today?' Mansur asked. His accent was so pronounced, thick with a rolling flourish, that Hamid wondered if it was intended as a joke. 'What a beautiful smell you have, such perfume! A voice like *zuwarde* and a body like a gazelle. Tell me, *msichana*, what time are you free tonight? I need someone to massage my back.'

The girl ignored him. With his back to them, Hamid heard Mansur continue to chat to the girl, singing wild praises to her while he tried to fix a time. In his confusion Hamid could not find a tin of polish. When he turned round with it at last, he thought she had been watching him all the time, and was amused that he had been so flustered. He smiled, but she frowned and then paid him. Mansur was talking beside her, cajoling and flattering, rattling the coins in his jacket pocket, but she turned and left without a word.

'Look at her, as if the sun itself wouldn't dare shine on her. So proud! But the truth is she's easy meat,' Mansur said, his body gently rocking with suppressed laughter. 'I'll be having that one before long. How much do you think she'll take? They always do that, these women, all these airs and disgusted looks . . . but once you've got them into bed, and you've got inside them, then they know who's the master.'

Hamid found himself laughing, keeping the peace among men. But he did not think she was a girl to be purchased. She was so certain and comfortable in every action that he could not believe her abject enough for Mansur's designs. Again and again his mind returned to the girl, and when he was alone he imagined himself intimate with her. At night after he had shut up the shop, he went to sit for a few minutes with the old man, Fajir, who owned the shop and lived in the back. He could no longer see to himself and very rarely asked to leave his bed. A woman who lived nearby came to see to him during the day, and took free groceries from the shop in return, but at night the ailing old man liked to have Hamid sit with him for a little while. The smell of the dying man perfumed the room while they talked. There was not usually much to say, a ritual of complaints about poor business and plaintive prayers for the return of health. Sometimes when his spirits were low, Fajir talked tearfully of death and the life which awaited him there. Then Hamid would take the old man to the toilet, make sure his chamber-pot was clean and empty, and leave him. Late into the night, Fajir would talk to himself, sometimes his voice rising softly to call out Hamid's name.

Hamid slept outside in the inner yard. During the rains he cleared a space in the tiny store and slept there. He spent his nights alone and never went out. It was well over a year since he had even left the shop, and before then he had only gone out with Fajir, before the old man was bedridden. Fajir had taken him to the mosque every Friday, and Hamid remembered the throngs of people and the cracked pavements steaming in the rain. On the way home they went to the market, and the old man named the luscious fruit and the brightly coloured vegetables for him, picking up some of them to make him smell or touch. Since his teens, when he first came to live in this town, Hamid had worked for the old man. Fajir gave him his board and he worked in the shop. At the end of every day, he spent his nights alone, and often thought of his father and his mother, and the town of his birth. Even though he was no longer a boy, the memories made him weep and he was degraded by the feelings that would not leave him be.

When the girl came to the shop again, to buy beans and sugar, Hamid was generous with the measures. She noticed and smiled at him. He beamed with pleasure, even though he knew that her smile was laced with derision. The next time she actually said something to him, only a greeting, but spoken pleasantly. Later she told him that her name was Rukiya and that she had recently moved into the area to live with relatives.

'Where's your home?' he asked.

'Mwembemaringo,' she said, flinging an arm out to indicate that it was a long way away. 'But you have to go on back-roads and over hills.'

He could see from the blue cotton dress she wore during the day that she worked as a domestic. When he asked her where she worked, she snorted softly first, as if to say that the question was unimportant. Then she told him that until she could find something better, she was a maid at one of the new hotels in the city.

'The best one, the Equator,' she said. 'There's a swimming pool and carpets everywhere. Almost everyone staying there is a *mzungu*, a European. We have a few Indians too, but none of these people from the bush who make the sheets smell.'

He took to standing at the doorway of his backyard bedchamber after he had shut the shop at night. The streets were empty and silent at that hour, not the teaming, dangerous places of the day. He thought of Rukiya often, and sometimes spoke her name, but thinking of her only made him more conscious of his isolation and squalor. He remembered how she had looked to him the first time, moving away in the late evening shadow. He wanted to touch her . . . Years in darkened places had done this to him, he thought, so that now he looked out on the streets of the foreign town and imagined that the touch of an unknown girl would be his salvation.

One night he stepped out into the street and latched the door behind him. He walked slowly towards the nearest street-lamp, then to the one after that. To his surprise he did not feel frightened. He heard something move but he did not look. If he did not know where he was going, there was no need to fear since anything could happen. There was comfort in that.

He turned a corner into a street lined with shops, one or two of which were lit, then turned another corner to escape the lights. He had not seen anyone, neither a policeman nor a night watchman. On the edge of a square he sat for a few minutes on a wooden bench, wondering that everything should seem so familiar. In one corner was a clock tower, clicking softly in the silent night. Metal posts lined the sides of the square, impassive and correct. Buses were parked in rows at one end, and in the distance he could hear the sound of the sea.

He made for the sound, and discovered that he was not far from the waterfront. The smell of the water suddenly made him think of his father's home. That town too had been by the sea, and once he had played on the beaches and in the shallows like all the other children. He no longer thought of it as somewhere he belonged to, somewhere that was his home. The water lapped gently at the foot of the sea-wall, and he stopped to peer at it breaking into white froth against the concrete. Lights were still shining brightly on one of the jetties and there was a hum of mechanical activity. It did not seem possible that anyone could be working at that hour of the night.

There were lights on across the bay, single isolated dots that were strung across a backdrop of darkness. Who lived there? he wondered. A shiver of fear ran through him. He tried to picture people living in that dark corner of the city. His mind gave him images of strong men with cruel faces, who peered at him and laughed. He saw dimly lit clearings where shadows lurked in wait for the stranger, and where later, men and women crowded over the body. He heard the sound of their feet pounding in an old ritual, and heard their cries of triumph as the blood of their enemies flowed into the pressed earth. But it was not only for the physical threat they posed that he feared the people who lived in the dark across the bay. It was because they knew where they were, and he was in the middle of nowhere.

He turned back towards the shop, unable to resist, despite everything, a feeling that he had dared something. It became a habit that after he had shut up the shop at night and had seen to Fajir, he went for a stroll to the waterfront. Fajir did not like it and complained about being left alone, but Hamid ignored his grumbles. Now and then he saw people, but they hurried past without a glance. During the day, he kept an eye out for the girl who now so filled his hours. At night he imagined himself with her. As he strolled the silent streets, he tried to think she was there with him, talking and smiling, and sometimes putting the palm of her hand on his neck. When she came to the shop, he always put in something extra, and waited for her to smile. Often they spoke, a few words of greeting and friendship. When there were shortages he served her from the secret reserves he kept for special customers. Whenever he dared he complimented her on her appearance, and squirmed with longing and confusion when she rewarded him with radiant smiles. Hamid laughed to himself as he remembered Mansur's boast about the girl. She was no girl to be bought with a few shillings, but one to be sung to, to be won with display and courage. And neither Mansur, half-blind with shit as he was, nor Hamid, had the words or the voice for such a feat.

Late one evening, Rukiya came to the shop to buy sugar. She was still in her blue work-dress, which was stained under the arms with sweat. There were no other customers, and she did not seem in a hurry. She began to tease him gently, saying something about how hard he worked.

'You must be very rich after all the hours you spend in the shop. Have you got a hole in the yard where you hide your money? Everyone knows shopkeepers have secret hoards . . . Are you saving to return to your town?'

'I don't have anything,' he protested. 'Nothing here belongs to me.'

She chuckled disbelievingly. 'But you work too hard, anyway,' she said. 'You don't have enough fun.' Then she smiled as he put in an additional scoopful of sugar.

'Thank you,' she said, leaning forward to take the package from him. She stayed that way for a moment longer than necessary, then she moved back slowly. 'You're always giving me things. I know you'll want something in return. When you do, you'll have to give me more than these little gifts.'

Hamid did not reply, overwhelmed with shame. The girl laughed lightly and moved away. She glanced round once, grinning at him before she plunged into the darkness.

SAIDA HAGI-DIRIE HERZI

Government by magic spell

At the village

When she was ten, Halima learned that she was possessed by a jinni. The diagnosis came from the religious healer of the village, the Wadaad. Halima had been ill for several months. The Wadaad had tried all his healing arts on her till he had understood that there could be no cure: Halima was not ill in the ordinary sense of the word; she was possessed – possessed by the spirit of an infant, which she had stepped on by accident, one night in front of the bathroom. Fortunately for Halima, the sage expounded, the jinni was of the benevolent sort, one that was more likely to help than to harm her. But it would never leave her – not leave her voluntarily, not even yield to exorcism. And it would forever be an infant jinni.

With that Halima became famous. The story of her jinni was known from one end of the village to the other within hours after the Wadaad had told her mother. Everyone talked about Halima and her jinni – what it might do and what it might be made to do, for her and for the village. In no time at all, the villagers had convinced themselves and each other that Halima had the power to foretell the future and to heal the sick. And it was not long before Halima herself was convinced.

Before long, Halima began to act the part. At times she would sit staring off into space. People assumed that she was listening to her jinni. Or she would actually go into a trance – she would talk, though no one was there to talk to; she would shout at the top of her voice and sometimes she would even cry. Those who witnessed these scenes were filled with holy dread. All were careful not to disturb Halima, during those moments or at any other time, for fear that they might offend the jinni. If people talked about Halima they did so in whispers, behind her back.

Halima made believe that the spirits of the infant's parents visited her during those moments of trance. They came to enquire of the infant, she told people, came to teach her how she could make the jinni happy. At the same time, Halima affirmed, they told her all manner of things about life in general, about the people of the village, things past, things present and things yet to come.

A question that was on the minds of many people in the village was who was to marry Halima when she reached the marriageable age. No one doubted that she would marry. It was what women were for – marriage and childbearing. But there was the problem of the jinni. Wouldn't it be dangerous to be married to a woman possessed? Would there be men brave enough to want to marry Halima?

When Halima did reach the marriageable age, a problem presented itself which no one had anticipated. Halima did not *want* to get married. There were indeed men brave enough to want to marry her, but Halima turned them all down. The Wadaad himself proposed to her. He, people thought, would have been the ideal husband for Halima: he, if anyone, should have been able to cope with a woman possessed. But Halima turned him down too.

Not that possession by a jinni spirit was something unusual in Halima's village. Stories of jinnis abounded – of people who were actually possessed by jinnis, of people who had jinni spirits that were like invisible twin brothers, or people who had jinni spirits as servants. It was common knowledge that one of Halima's own forefathers had had a jinni twin brother called Gess Ade, and one of her mother's grandfathers had had, in addition to a jinni twin brother, three devoted jinni servants called Toore, Gaadale, and Toor-Ourmone respectively. When Halima's mother had problems, she called on those three for help and protection. The ancestors of several clans were believed to have been born twins, a jinni being the twin partner of each of them. The tribe of Halima's brother-in-law had a twin jinni by the name of Sarhaan.

When animals were sacrificed, the jinni twins had to get their share. In return, the jinnis were expected to give support and protection to the clan. First the animals would be butchered. Then, the ritual songs having been sung, the carcasses would be cut open and the inner organs removed. These were to be given to the jinnis. Admonitions would be mumbled such as 'Let's not forget Gess Ade's share; or Toore's, Gaadale's, Ourmone's . . .'

The parts set aside for the jinnis would be taken to a remote place up in the hills, and, because they invariably and mysteriously disappeared, the villagers were sure that the jinnis devoured them. No one, therefore, would dream of cheating the jinnis of their share. This had been so for generations and would continue to be so. Children were made to memorise the ritual songs so as to keep the ancestral rites intact from generation to generation.

When Halima was under the spell of her spirits, all her emotions seemed intensified. She experienced a feeling of power, as though she could do things beyond the reach of ordinary human beings. She felt good then. Moreover, whatever she undertook, her spirits seemed to lend a helping hand. Because the fortunes of her family, indeed those of the whole clan, prospered at the time, Halima as well as other people assumed that it was the spirits' doing. In time, Halima came to be regarded as a blessing to her family, an asset to the whole clan. And she gloried in the special status her spirits gave her.

To the capital

It was because of her special powers that Halima was summoned to the capital. A big part of her clan was there. The most important and the most powerful positions in the government were held by people of her clan. It had all started with one of their men, who had become very powerful in the government. He had called his relatives and found big government jobs for them. They in turn had called relatives of theirs till the government had virtually been taken over by Halima's people. And that had meant quick riches for everyone concerned. Nor had they been very scrupulous about getting what they wanted: anything that had stood in their way had been pushed aside or eliminated. At the time when Halima was summoned, her clan controlled the government and with that the wealth of the country so completely that no one dared to challenge them any more and they could get away with murder. Still they wanted to secure for themselves the extra protection of Halima's supernatural powers.

They had tried to get Halima's father to come to the capital as well. He was a man of stature, whose presence would have done honour to the clan. But he did not want to go. Old and resentful of change, he did not want to leave the peace and security of his village for the madness of the big city. But he was also afraid for his reputation. It was solid in his village but joining this gang might tarnish it, something he did not want to risk so near the end of his life. However, though he did not want to go himself, he had no reservations about sending his son and his daughter there. On one hand he hoped that they might get a slice of the big pie for themselves and so for the family. On the other hand he thought it would do no harm to have Halima there to protect the clan and to ensure its continued domination. Perhaps she could come to a deal with her spirits – she to continue looking after their infant and they to look after the welfare of the clan.

Halima did let herself be persuaded to go, but, before she went, she consulted her spirits. They asked her to perform two rituals. One was to prepare 'Tahleel', a special type of water, over which certain rituals were performed. People drank it or bathed in it to benefit from its powers. The second was to perform daily annual sacrifices to Gess Ade, the clan's twin spirit. Select parts of the innards of thousands of animals – hearts, kidneys, intestines and others – were to be offered to him every day on the eastern shore.

When Halima and her brother were ready to go, a cousin of theirs came from the big city to fetch them. From this cousin, who was an important government official, the two learned many things. They learned about the great privileges their people enjoyed in the city. They got an idea what wealth they had amassed since the clan had come 'to power'. They found out how completely the clan was in control of the government. They were awed, the more so when their informant told them that the clan had 'achieved' all this greatness in ten short years and that most of the people who now held important government positions were illiterate.

In the big city

In the city, the two were given a beautiful villa complete with lots of servants and security guards. Within days, Halima's brother obtained an important government position of his own. He was made the head of the department that handled the sale of all incense, both inside and outside the country. Its official name was Government Incense Agency.

And Halima wasted no time carrying out the two requests of her spirits. She asked two things from the leaders of the clan. She asked them to bring all the water resources of the city together in one central pool to facilitate the performing of the 'Tahleel' and she requested the building of a huge slaughterhouse at the eastern shore. The leaders readily granted her requests since they were convinced that Halima's ministrations were of crucial importance for the continued success of the clan.

To centralise the city's water system, two huge water reservoirs were created, one in the eastern half and one in the western half of the city. Eventually all the wells of the city were destroyed, even the ones in private houses, and all water systems were connected to the two reservoirs. This way all the water consumed in the city came from the same source, and when Halima put the spell of her 'Tahleel' on the two reservoirs, it reached everyone.

One of the effects of the 'Tahleel' was to cure people of curiosity. Those who drank it stopped asking questions. Above all they stopped wondering about the actions of the clan's leading men. They became model subjects doing without question, without objection, what they were told to do. And Halima kept putting ever new spells on the water, faster than the old ones wore off. Though no one but she herself knew what kind of magic she put on the water, rumours abounded. One rumour had it that she performed certain incantations over the bath water of the leader and then released it into the reservoirs. There was no doubt in her mind and in the minds of the leaders that as long as everyone drank the water that carried her 'Tahleel' everything would go according to their plans.

When the new slaughterhouse went into operation, all other slaughterhouses were closed down. Unfortunately the new slaughterhouse was close to the Lido, the most popular of the city's beaches. In no time at all, the waters off the Lido swarmed with man-eating sharks, drawn there by the waste of blood and offals discharged by the slaughterhouse. After a number of people had been killed by the predators people stopped going to the Lido. There was no comment from the government. Quite obviously the slaughterhouse, where the sacrifices to Gess Ade were performed, was more important to the rulers of the country than the beach.

Every so often Halima would come to the slaughterhouse to check on the performance of the animal sacrifices. Here too she modified the rituals periodically to strengthen their effect.

As things kept going well for the tribe and her, Halima became more and more sure that she was the cause of it all. The clan's leaders too were convinced that they owed their continued success to Halima and her spirits. They heaped honours on her. They consulted her on all important issues and her counsel often proved invaluable. It was Halima, for instance, who thought up the idea of the shortages to keep the common people subdued. Shortages of all basic commodities were deliberately created and they kept people busy struggling for bare survival. They did not have time or energy to spare worrying about the goings-on in the government. The leaders of the clan felt more secure than ever.

Nearly twenty years have passed since Halima first went to the city. She is still performing her rituals, and the affairs of the clan are still prospering. Its men still hold all the important posts in the government and they still control the wealth of the country. As for the rest of the nation – they are mostly struggling to make ends meet, something that's becoming more and more difficult. And if there should be a few that might have time and energy left to start asking questions, Halima's Tahleel and her various other forms of magic take care of them. The men of the clan continue to govern with the help of Halima's magic spell.

TOLOLWA MARTI MOLLEL

A night out

For a long moment, Mika sat awkwardly, without his usual self-assurance, despite the alcohol singing in his veins. But suddenly, feeling a fool for his unease, he cleared his throat, a trifle too loudly, and ventured: 'What's your name?'

'Mama Tumaini.' (Mother of Tumaini)

She did not lift her eyes but went on busying herself with putting the child to sleep on the mat on the floor. Quite unexpectedly, the child began to cough, a violent, racking outburst that threw his little body into spasms.

Mika leaned forward and felt the child. His brow was damp and hot with fever. 'Has he had treatment?' he asked, relieved to find something neutral to say.

She replied, 'There isn't an aspirin to be had at the dispensary.'

Under the mother's soothing, the child Tumaini eventually lay still, asleep, his breath rasping in and out. Mama Tumaini wrapped herself in a *khanga*, then lit a mosquito coil. Smoke rose in spiral, spreading over the mat. The child stirred and sneezed. The mother, squatting gently patted him to sleep.

'God grant you health, my little one,' she murmured, 'God grant you health and strength, good little mama's soldier!'

'Why soldier . . .?' Mika asked, rather pointlessly.

'Yes, soldiers don't starve, or get sick.' She spoke with such toneless simplicity, it could have been a child talking.

'Yes, they don't starve,' Mika said, 'they get killed!'

'Better to die than this nameless misery of ours,' she shot back. 'Better a quick clean bullet in the head than this slow dying and burning from hunger and disease!'

'Oh, soldiers starve too, you know, when there is nothing to eat . . .', Mika said hard-heartedly.

But she was sunk deep in her thoughts, she might not have heard. Then as if to herself, alone in the room, she said, 'Tumaini's father was a soldier . . .'

'Was . . .?' went Mika.

'. . . a real bull of a man he was, with none to equal him. Life was easier then, with him around. He was like a father to me, to my mother, to all of us. Now living has become such a task. You have to struggle for each small thing. Everything, everything, you have to pay for in blood, if you can find it! If Tumaini's father were around still . . .' She seemed almost on the point of bursting into tears, but she didn't.

'Why, is he dead?' Mika asked, but purely out of curiosity, his voice too loud and untouched by the woman's dull sorrow.

'I don't want to talk, don't ask me, please . . .' she pleaded, then she began to cry and said through her tears. 'He went off to Uganda, to war. He might be alive, he might be dead . . .'

Mika said nothing. The child Tumaini was still again, his mother's hand on him, still patting, absently. At last Mama Tumaini straightened up and turned off the small tin lamp in the room. In the dark, she submitted herself, silently, dutifully, and professionally. But, afterwards, when Mika rolled his body off her, there wasn't the usual feeling of having conquered; though fully sated, he lay back less than happy, vaguely unsettled, the laboured breathing from the mat adding to his sense of deflation.

He did not know when he finally fell asleep and woke up with the panic of one who does not know where he is. It was not until he felt Mama Tumaini's body by his side that he remembered where he was.

He got out of bed and lit a cigarette. The coil had burnt out and mosquitoes buzzed angrily. He sat frowning in the dark, something troubling him, though he didn't know what. Suddenly he was aware of the silence in the room.

Mouth dry and head faintly throbbing, he got up, putting out his cigarette, and went to the mat. There was no sound from the child and in the darkness he could only make out a mute, still haze, but he dared not strike a match to light the lamp. He put his hand out towards the child, and his eyes, gradually used to the dark, gazed down fascinated at the little body, lifeless and cold to his touch, its form now becoming distinct under the first stabs of dawnlight.

Mama Tumaini stirred, mumbled something, then went back to sleep. Mika waited until her breathing grew deep and even again before he sat on the bed, gingerly, and lit another cigarette, his mind busy.

Then, moving softly, he picked up his clothes from the floor where he had dumped them in a drunken pile. Dressed, he paused awhile, his eyes involuntarily seeking the child's body. No, he must leave immediately, he urged himself. It wouldn't do to get caught in the mourning and the funeral ceremonies. There was no point and it would delay him further. And anyway, he found himself thinking, what was the child to him, or the mother for that matter? Mechanically, he took out his wallet, peeled off several notes, and with no attempt to make out the amount, placed the money on a stool by the bed, and set the lamp on it as weight.

The door squeaked as he unbolted it. He paused, his heart pounding, his ear strained towards the bed.

Mama Tumaini stirred. 'You're going already?' she asked him.

'Yes,' he answered.

'This early?'

'You know that transport is a problem, and I have to travel today.'

●

Come what may, he just had to get out today, and try and make it to Dar es Salaam by nightfall. For two days now, he had been sunk in this dreary little town, because petrol shortage had crippled transportation and inundated the small town with stranded travellers. It was to get away from the sweating hordes hopelessly milling all over the town in search of transport, that on the previous day he had decided on an evening of entertainment and action. Drink had appealed to him as just the antidote he needed for his despondence. But the search for beer, which he preferred, was doomed from the start. There had been no beer in town, he was told at the first bar he stopped in, since the day the beer truck went crashing over a bridge leading into town. The truck was still here, a useless wreck of scrap metal. Mika did not want to believe this although he suspected it was probably the truth. He would have given his little finger for a drop of beer, and he went all over town, which didn't take long as there was little of it besides the bus stop.

A couple of depressing, dusty, narrow lanes made up the backbone of the town and beyond that was only a patchwork of slums. But he had no luck whatever in his search and had to make do with the local *pombe* which was in abundance. He had little stomach for local stuff, but even though he imbibed it slowly and grudgingly, gradually the booze took hold and he felt some of his despair lift. He even felt cheerful enough to join a group of local drinkers at a nearby table. But just as the evening seemed to be taking off, he suddenly found himself abandoned, his fellow drinkers having left for other bars or their homes. He had left too, and gone stumbling through the night. He would never remember how he ended up in Mama Tumaini's place, or why he decided he could not spend the night alone in his bed in the room he had rented at the lodging house. Funny, he thought aimlessly, paying for a room then sleeping elsewhere; wasteful, he concluded grimly.

Mama Tumaini was talking. 'Even so,' she said, 'won't you wait for me to make you a cup of tea at least, to start you off?' That was the last thing he wanted, her getting up and finding out about the baby. He had to get away first. 'No, no,' he said quickly, 'my things are at the lodging house, I've to get ready. I'll eat somewhere.'

'Suit yourself,' she said, turning over. Then faintly, almost inaudibly, as if it was an afterthought, she wished him a safe journey.

He thanked her, then limply, guiltily, he mumbled, 'Your money . . . I've put the money . . . your money . . . on the stool.' But she might have gone back to sleep or she might have had enough of him, as she made no response.

Mika opened the door and walked away in quick, tense steps, as light broke out over the rooftops and wisps of smoke from the early morning cooking lazed over the slums, announcing the start of another day.

KYALO MATIVO

On the market day

Kamali Lango woke up in the midst of the night, long before the village owl. Kokia, his wife, was already up and his food was ready: a maize meal – yesterday's left-overs – which was re-warmed in boiling water, a cup of grade-two hot coffee with a touch of powdered milk, and sour milk. He ate with relish.

He ate to a powerful munching silence. The open-air kerosene can-lamp, fondly baptised Shike-n'tandike, flapped its flame noisily as if in a concerted effort to break the uncomfortable silence, and the embers on the hearth cracked in positive response. It was a familiar cracking.

One of the young ones stirred, and the parents froze. The father stopped chewing, and the mother held her breath . . . If only there was a way of destroying that dangerous smell of food . . . But the young one merely turned on his other side and fell back into sleep. That was all.

'Remember, my mother is coming here the day after the day after tomorrow,' Kokia said almost in a whisper. There was no immediate answer; he knew only too well what was on the agenda. But he had to respond in one way or another.

'Yes, I know.'

'What should I do then?'

'I intend to be back by then.'

'And if not?'

The wife was not given to prying. But in trying times vagueness is a crime.

'The day after the day after tomorrow is not yet here,' he said defensively. 'There is no cause for hysteria,' he continued. 'We are not yet trashed; so we can still find a way out. Have you joined those hopeless people who go around shouting, "we shall not survive, we shall not survive, this is the end of the tether . . . this is the . . ."?' The words threatened to choke in his throat. And an obstinate sonorous echo continued to ring in his mind like an alarm clock: '. . . is the end of the tether . . . the end of the tether . . . end of the tether . . . of the tether . . . .'

It was indeed the end of the tether. At least as far as that unpleasant conversation was concerned. So he stood up, picked up his wrapped-up blanket, his stick, his small torch, and stepped out into the dark and silent night. From across the Wingoo Valley, the faint and lonely wailing of a dog came riding the air current.

After a reflective interval, the mother lifted up the can-lamp and held it above her head as she bent to survey the young ones. Then she put out the flame and went back to sleep.

All that was routine. Last week she did the same. The week before last, she did the same. Last year, when she had only seven children, it was the same thing. And at the end of the year, when her ninth child begins to walk, she will do it again.

The man was counting his fingers as he groped his way through the dark. Well, he knew his way quite well, he has walked the same path for . . . now let's see . . . three . . . four? No, five years at least. Somehow, even during the darkest of the nights he managed to find his way. 'The sun always rises, even if not always to the Glory of God.' That was his magic wand, his consolation. But a consolation.

Last year, he reckoned, he made, ooh, let's see . . . eh . . . about . . . one . . . or . . . Yes, one hundred shillings net. He lost how many cattle? . . . The spotted one, the sharp-horned heifer, the brown bull, the white-crowned cow, the black-topped . . . the . . . that's all. Or? Yes, that's all. Nevertheless . . . Nevertheless, the sun always rises 'even if not always to the Glory of God'. This year, if all goes well, 'I mean if the rains fall . . .' he paused for a while to wrestle with an agonising memory. 'There used to be a thick forest here, saturated with life . . . and now all that remains is a dry whirlwind . . . Anyway this year if the rains come I could make as much as, ooh, two hundred, three hundred . . .' But he stopped there. There was this disturbing memory, you see, that for the last two years, if he could remember well – and it was a curse to have to remember – there had been no rain, not even an imitation of it. And two or three days ago Radio Wananchi reminded the people that lack of rain, and therefore famine, are natural phenomena against which man is powerless. It added: 'Let that be known to those who are accusing the government of doing nothing; let them know that their rumour-mongering will not be tolerated.'

Kamali Lango had bought himself a transistor radio two . . . three rainy seasons ago to keep abreast with the times. And that night after the message had been relayed to the people, the peasants echoed it back and forth in the usual manner, nodding their heads to the truth of the broadcast and beating their breasts cursing the harsh, invisible and uncontrollable power so magnificently blamed by the broadcast: nature. Naturally it was their fault for failing to come together to gather the necessary money for a water project. Every fool knew it. But one thing was clear: the weather broadcasts had long ceased to bear the summarised forecasts of cold spells and low clouds. They had long turned into out-and-out political commentaries exonerating the government of the people, freely chosen in the most becoming and the latest democratic fashion in the world.

Dawn.

Down the footpath the man had gone quite a distance by now. The first glimmer of light found him still tramping; but not alone. After every other kilometre or so he met a line of villagers from beyond the mountains marching their donkeys in the opposite direction to fetch drinking-water. It was known that these villagers spent four days to accomplish that mission. And the old ones say it was the first time they had known that to happen. Ah well, it was rumour-mongering. But then so what? As the famous broadcast so aptly put it, 'you don't expect things to fall down like manna'.

'Greetings!'

'How do you fare?'

'Well. Only you.'

'And the people.'

The people – Hmm, sorry – the people are well too.

Day-break.

The naked sun rose slowly and surely, an accursed red ball of ill-will. For days on end, it had risen in the same manner behind the same mountain. Sure enough, another day-break. And there, all around him, rose a sea of dust, stretching far and beyond the sky-line. It was a familiar sight and the man had long ceased to take note of it. His feet, covered with red soil, carried him triumphantly as they had always done countless times before. He cocked up his head on one side and sent a couple of bullets of spittle hurtling through the air. There was still enough saliva left all right. And when the times are good, a morning like this welcomes him like a ruling monarch; yes, it washes his feet with dew, and the clean air cleanses his foul breath. He shook his head as if to rid himself of an unpleasant thought. It was then, when he lifted his head, that he found out that actually he no longer had the monopoly of the path. He was walking ahead of and behind an ever-growing line of other people, all like him trying to beat the deadline of the tyrannical sun. The line of the people grew longer and longer, and soon there was a steady flow of men and women. Now the path was a sprightly scene of dust from which silence was banished. A spontaneous murmur came into being, changing slowly into a buzz. Jingles joined, and out of this combination a rhythm was born. There was chanting and whistling. The songleader was a fly-whisk-wielding home-made poet in his own right. He marched in the very front of the line and dished out doses of the countryside's pride, and the men joined in at the prescribed intervals while the women provided the chorus. The current song was in praise of a young man who had collected all kinds of degrees from all over the world, but who returned to his native home on foot. White civilisation had failed to annex him. He had come home to serve the people in any capacity they would assign to him. The circumstances of this young man's beautiful history were once again unfolded in the song, and all natural elements bore witness to them:

> *LEADER*
> *When the moon shines*
> *It is because Mbula is out there*
> *Visiting the people;*
>
> *When the wind blows*
> *It is because Mbula*
> *Is there caring for the sick;*

When the sun rises
It is because Mbula
Rose up early to attend to the young;

So what do you say?

CHORUS
We have heard his footsteps
Shuffling among the reeds
And on the countryside on rainy days
We have seen his deeds;

And we have felt his tears
Trickling on our cheeks:

ALL
And he will feed the hungry
For he is the son of the country.

It was high season. Everybody knew what that meant. Even Kamali Lango couldn't quite plead innocent of it. Events were galloping to a head in the muddy arena of politics. And so was this procession. And so was the heat of the sun. And shortly they would be there.

Pancreas Mbula was already there. Unlike his opponents, he was the first to arrive. A few other people had already arrived too, but serious business hadn't begun until the group had been reinforced by the new recruits. Then he stood up and spoke about the main points of his programme: free education, free medicine, provision of irrigation projects and establishment of clinics and nursery schools in the villages where the people lived.

'But,' he went on, 'there is no substitute for self-help. We have to start somewhere, and the main force will come from you. On my part, I shall do, as I have always done, what I can to contribute to a fair social set-up. I shall persuade the government to allocate some money to these projects. I pledge myself and promise, as sure as I stand here now, to serve you with all my heart. Indeed I'm aware of what the previous Member of Parliament did during the term of his office; he abused the privilege you bestowed on him, and instead of representing you, he represented himself, his family and his close circle of friends.

Ten years ago he entered the Parliament as poor as a butterfly, but ten years later he left it a fat maggot of a millionaire. And that is not all: he has the shamelessness to campaign for another term of office!'

A thunderous applause.

'I say it again as I have done several times before: the real power rests with you. Your votes are too precious to give away to a blood-sucking parasite. Let it be your choice that I be the next MP for Ngangani, and I tell you, before the end of two years, you yourselves will be the witnesses of change. If in two years no changes have occurred, then you have the right to come and say so to my face. I will deserve to be removed without hesitation.'

'What will you do about the lack of rain, son?' the tired voice of a widower demanded from the crowd.

'Well,' he cleared his throat, 'you have all heard the story on the radio about the lack of rain being a natural catastrophe. Right now, we are sitting on a pool of water, and on both sides we are flanked by two perennial rivers. Lift up your eyes,' he said, pointing away, 'do you all see that mountain towering about the clouds with a white cap on top of it? Well, that "cap" is actually a frozen lake whose water melts four times every year and trickles down the mountain-sides right through the thick forest surrounding it, zigzagging its way down the slopes. That melted water is equal to twice as much water again as we receive from natural rain. Indeed with that much water we can turn this semi-desert into a green field all year round. And we have the will and the energy for that . . .'

Another applause went out from the crowd.

'Whoever doubts that, doubts the power of the people . . .'

Another applause.

'. . . And I'm asking only to be blessed with your votes, your valuable votes, in order to make this dream a reality.'

The ecstatic crowd broke into the chant:

> *We have heard his footsteps*
> *Shuffling among the weeds,*
> *And on the countryside on rainy days*
> *We have seen his deeds;*

And we have felt his tears
Trickling on our cheeks:

And he will feed the hungry
For he is the son of the country.

For Kamali Lango it was a familiar event processed in a familiar manner. He had seen and heard it all before and, like all others, had waited for the promised changes, and was still waiting. He left the scene of political action and continued on his journey.

It was now midday.

The market place was bursting with pompous peasant pride, a splendid scene of swarming flies, scorching sun, mooing cows and bellowing bulls. And from time to time, in the midst of this motley of noise, a sharp cry of agony would be heard. It was the cry of a baby demanding what in the circumstances was a simple impossibility: food. He walked right through the market from the western to the eastern section of it, until he arrived at the most familiar of all the familiar scenes: the cattle shed.

The auction was already in full swing. The smell of dung, the ceaseless mooing of the cattle, the yelling of the merchants and the boiling earth, all added to the atmosphere of cut-throat competition which brought the men into a beard-to-beard confrontation. And wielding your dagger, you stabbed and got stabbed, for it was the nature of the trade.

'There goes a majestic family bull . . . Look how he strides; what a public show of strength.' It was the auction master announcing the next candidate for raucous bidding.

'Two hundred,' shouted a prospective buyer.

'Two hundred,' repeated the auction master.,

'Two hundred and fifty,' came a challenging voice.

'Two hundred and fifty . . . two hundred and fifty . . .'

'Three hundred,' yet another bidder.

'Four hundred.'

'Four hundred . . . four hundred . . . FOUR HUNDRED. The purchase has been made,' concluded the auction master.

Kamali Lango meditated for a while. He wasn't sure any more now whether he could participate in the bidding without running a risk. But then that's exactly what the thing amounted to: risk. Meanwhile another bull was put up.

'. . . A healthy animal of beefy elegance,' the master eulogised.

'Three hundred . . . three hundred . . .'

'Four hundred . . ., four hundred . . .'

'Five hundred . . ., five hundred . . .; five . . .'

'Six hundred,' a billy-goat-like voice pierced the air with a malicious intent. That was Menge. The audience let out a murmur of indifference. The new bidder was the renowned local cattle-dealer, rumoured to possess the capability to sweep out all the cattle in stock within and outside the community at any given moment. In matters of trade, his word was final. Everybody knew it. But as a matter of formality, the auction master proceeded to make the count-down. And as he did so, a wiry, wind-blown weakling climbed down the buyers' platform and wound his way to the centre of the bargaining shed. Aware of his financial power, Menge began to drive the animal out of the shed long before the count-down was over.

'SEVEN HUNDRED!'

It wasn't just the noise which startled some people, sent others choking with laughter and left others numb. It was simply the unexpected turn of events. It was so devastating that Menge's stick fell down from his hand. He stood still for a moment like one who had been shot in the back with an arrow, then picked up his stick and walked back to the buyers' platform. He needed simply to shout 'one thousand' to silence every prospective challenger. But he wasn't going to acept a challenge from a nondescript peasant. No, he dismissed the challenge with contempt. Meanwhile the auction master had finished the count, and, like a skilful hunter that he felt himself to be at this moment, Kamali Lango stepped down and marched proudly to collect his prey. All watched him walk across the bargaining shed as he drove his new deal out.

Then he went to the cashier's desk and counted seven hundred shillings from his pocket. It was all he had.

Seven hundred shillings was his life-savings, his working capital for five years. Now that it had changed into a four-legged commodity for self-expansion, he ought to get added value of . . . ooh, . . . one . . . two hundred shillings? Who knows? Maybe more, maybe less. But he didn't need to worry about that; it wasn't the first time it had happened to him. Now, as before, there was always the rising sun.

Twilight.

That night, as always, Kamali Lango stayed with a friend of his who lived mid-way between the buying and the selling market. By sunset the next day he would go to the selling market. After selling his bull, he planned to catch a bus leaving for his home that evening. But he would get off at Kaimu market to buy two sacks of maize and then wait for the midnight bus from the coast. He would load his two sacks of maize in it and travel to Kamulamba, the country-bus station nearest to his home where his wife and three other women would be waiting. They would unload the maize, tear the sacks open and transfer the contents to three smaller baskets. They would all carry the maize home. At home his mother-in-law would be waiting. He would give her some of the maize, pay the three women with two cans full of grain each and keep the rest for his family. The supply should keep his family going until the next trip.

It was a familiar pattern. Nothing new, nothing eventful.

Dusk.

His bull behaved well and apparently didn't need a lot to eat. He gave it some grass he had been carrying for the purpose. They walked all day, the man and the animal, until they were both exhausted by the heat. So he decided to stop under a tree for a short rest. He tied the animal to a nearby twig and lay down for a small nap. The quietness of the place lulled him into a deep sleep. How long it had lasted he couldn't quite tell. When he woke up the animal was still there but this time he was also lying down. Well, it was time to go on, so he untethered the animal and patted it on the back.

'Hey, up up we go.'

The animal didn't budge. So he hit it slightly with a stick.

'Up, up, I say . . . Get going.'

The animal remained immobile. He hit it harder. Still the animal didn't move. He grabbed its ears and pulled them. That didn't help either. He gave it two or three canes on the back. Then the animal lay on its back and began to kick in the air with froth coming from its mouth.

Kamali Lango dropped his luggage and hurried to open the animal's mouth. That proved to be quite a task. The animal gnashed its teeth and gave a groaning noise. Then there was silence.

It was a long while before the man picked up his remaining property: the stick, the torch, the wrapped-up blanket, and walked away. A battalion of vultures watched him go, and then inched nearer to the scene. They had been waiting impatiently all the while. Unlike the bull, these guardians of the sky had not succumbed yet to an epileptic fit.

Kamali Lango sombrely remembered that at Kamulamba his wife and three other women would be waiting with three baskets. He trudged home in bemused, wobbly steps.

M. G. VASSANJI

Leaving

Kichwele Street was now Uhuru Street. My two sisters had completed school and got married and Mother missed them sometimes. Mehroon, after a succession of wooers, had settled for a former opening batsman of our school team and was in town. Razia was a wealthy housewife in Tanga, the coastal town north of Dar. Firoz dropped out in his last year at school, and everyone said that it was a wonder he had reached that far. He was assistant bookkeeper at Oriental Emporium, and brought home stationery sometimes.

Mother had placed her hopes on the youngest two of us, Aloo and me, and she didn't want us distracted by the chores that always needed doing around the store. One evening she secured for the last time the half a dozen assorted padlocks on the sturdy panelled doors and sold the store. This was exactly one week after the wedding party had driven off with a tearful Razia, leaving behind a distraught mother in the stirred-up dust of Uhuru Street.

We moved to the residential area of Upanga. After the bustle of Uhuru Street, our new neighbourhood seemed quiet. Instead of the racket of buses, bicycles and cars on the road, we now heard the croaking of frogs and the chirping of insects. Nights were haunting, lonely and desolate and took some getting used to. Upanga Road emptied after seven in the evening and the sidestreets became pitch dark, with no illumination. Much of the area was as yet uninhabited and behind the housing developments there were overgrown bushes, large, scary baobab trees, and mango and coconut groves.

Sometimes in the evenings, when Mother felt sad, Aloo and I would play two-three-five with her, a variation of whist for three people. I had entered the University by then and came back at weekends. Aloo was in his last year at school. He had turned out to be exceptionally bright in his studies – more so than we realised.

That year Mr Datoo, a former teacher from our school who was also a former student, returned from America for a visit. Mr Datoo had been a favourite with the boys. When he came he received a tumultuous welcome. For the next few days he toured the town like the Pied Piper followed by a horde of adulating students, one of whom was Aloo.

The exciting event inspired in Aloo the hope that not only might he be admitted to an American university, but he could also win a scholarship to go there. Throughout the rest of the year, therefore, he wrote to numerous universities, culling their names from books at the USIS, often simply at random or even only by the sounds of their names.

Mother's response to all these efforts was to humour him. She would smile. 'Your uncles in America will pay thousands of shillings just to send you to college,' she would say. Evidently she felt he was wasting his time, but he would never be able to say that he did not have all the support she could give him.

Responses to his enquiries started coming within weeks and a handful of them were guardedly encouraging. Gradually Aloo found out which were the better places, and which among them the truly famous. Soon a few catalogues arrived, all looking impressive. It seemed that the more involved he became with the application process, the more tantalising was the prospect of going to an American university. Even the famous places did not discourage him. He learnt of subjects he had never heard of before: genetics, cosmology, artificial intelligence: a whole universe was out there waiting for him if only he could reach it. He was not sure if he could, if he was good enough. He suffered periods of intense hope and hopeless despair.

Of course, Aloo was entitled to a place at the local university. At the end of the year, when the selections were announced in the papers, his name was on the list. But some bureaucratic hand, probably also corrupt, dealt out a future prospect for him that came as a shock. He had applied to study medicine, he was given a place in agriculture. An agricultural officer in a rural district somewhere was not what he wanted to become however patriotic he felt. He had never left the city except to go to the national parks once on a school trip.

When Aloo received a letter from the California Institute of Technology offering him a place with a scholarship, he was stupefied at first. He read and reread the letter, not believing what it seemed to be saying, afraid that he might be reading something into it. He asked me to read it for him. When he was convinced there was no possibility of a mistake he became elated.

'The hell I'll do agriculture!' he grinned.

But first he had to contend with Mother.

Mother was incredulous. 'Go, go,' she said, 'don't you eat my head, don't tease me!'

'But it's true!' he protested. 'They're giving me a scholarship!'

We were at the table – the three of us – and had just poured tea from the thermos. Mother sitting across from me stared at her saucer for a while then she looked up.

'Is it true?' she asked me.

'Yes, it's true,' I said. 'All he needs is to take 400 dollars pocket money with him.'

'How many shillings would that make?' she asked.

'About three thousand.'

'And how are we going to raise this three thousand shillings? Have you bought a lottery? And what about the ticket? Are they going to send you a ticket too?'

As she said this Aloo's prospects seemed to get dimmer. She was right, it was not a little money that he needed.

'Can't we raise a loan?' he asked. 'I'll work there. Yes, I'll work as a waiter. A waiter! – I know you can do it, I'll send the money back!'

'You may have uncles in America who would help you,' Mother told him, 'but no one here will.'

Aloo's shoulders sagged and he sat there toying with his cup, close to tears. Mother sat drinking from her saucer and frowning. The evening light came in from the window behind me and gave a glint to her spectacles. Finally she set her saucer down. She was angry.

'And why do you want to go away, so far from us? Is this what I raised you for – so you could leave me to go away to a foreign place? Won't you miss us, where you want to go? Do we mean so little to you? If something happens . . .'

Aloo was crying. A tear fell into his cup, his nose was running. 'So many kids go and return, and nothing happens to them . . . Why did you mislead me, then? Why did you let me apply if you didn't want me to go . . . why did you raise my hopes if only to dash them?' He raised his voice to her, the first time I saw him do it, and he was shaking.

He did not bring up the question again and he prepared himself for the agricultural college, waiting for the term to begin. At home he would slump on the sofa putting away a novel a day.

If the unknown bureaucrat at the Ministry of Education had been less arbitrary, Aloo would not have been so broken and Mother would not have felt compelled to try and do something for him.

A few days later, on a Sunday morning, she looked up from her sewing machine and said to the two of us: 'Let's go and show this letter to Mr Velji. He is experienced in these matters. Let's take his advice.'

Mr Velji was a former administrator of our school. He had a large egg-shaped head and a small compact body. With his large forehead and big black spectacles he looked the caricature of the archetypal wise man. He also had the bearing of one. The three of us were settled in his sitting-room chairs staring about us and waiting expectantly when he walked in stiffly, like a toy soldier, to welcome us.

'How are you, sister?' he said. 'What can I do for you?'

Aloo and I stood up respectfully as he sat down.

'We have come to you for advice . . .' Mother began.

'Speak, then,' he said jovially and sat back, joining his hands behind his head.

She began by giving him her history. She told him which family she was born in, which she had married into, how she had raised her kids when our father died. Common relations were discovered between our families. 'Now this one here,' she pointed at me, 'goes to university here, and *that* one wants to go to America. Show him the documents,' she commanded Aloo.

As if with an effort, Aloo pushed himself out of the sofa and slowly made his way to place the documents in Mr Velji's hands. Before he looked at them Mr Velji asked Aloo his result in the final exam.

At Aloo's answer, his eyes widened. 'Henh?' he said, 'All A's?'

'Yes,' replied Aloo, a little too meekly.

Mr Velji flipped the papers one by one, cursorily at first. Then he went over them more carefully. He looked at the long visa form with the carbon copies neatly bound behind the original; he read over the friendly letter from the Foreign Student Adviser; he was charmed by the letters of invitation from the fraternities. Finally he looked up, a little humbled.

'The boy is right,' he said. 'The university is good, and they are giving him a bursary. I congratulate you.'

'But what should I do?' asked Mother anxiously. 'What is your advice? Tell us what we should do.'

'Well,' said Mr Velji, 'it would be good for his education.' He raised his hand to clear his throat. Then he said, a little slowly: 'But if you send him, you will lose your son.

'It's a far place, America,' he concluded, wiping his hands briskly at the finished business. 'Now what will you have – tea? orange squash?'

His wife appeared magically to take orders.

'All the rich kids go every year and they are not lost,' muttered Aloo bitterly as we walked back home. Mother was silent.

That night she was at the sewing machine and Aloo was on the couch, reading. The radio was turned low and through the open front door a gentle breeze blew in to cool the sitting room. I was standing at the door. The banana tree and its offspring rustled outside, a car zoomed on the road, throwing shadows on neighbouring houses. A couple out for a stroll, murmuring, came into sight over the uneven hedge; groups of boys or girls chattered before dispersing for the night. The intermittent buzz of an electric motor escaped from mother's sewing machine. It was a little darker where she sat at the other end of the room from us.

Presently she looked up and said a little nonchalantly, 'At least show me what this university looks like – bring that book, will you?'

Mother had never seen the catalogue. She had always dismissed it, had never shown the least bit of curiosity about the place Aloo wanted so badly to visit. Now the three of us crowded around the glossy pages, pausing at pictures of the neoclassic façades and domes, columns towering over humans, students rushing about in a dither of activity, classes held on lush lawns in ample shade. It all looked so awesome and yet inviting.

'It's something, isn't it?' whispered Aloo, hardly able to hold back his excitement. 'They teach hundreds of courses there,' he said. 'They send rockets into space . . . to other worlds . . . to the moon – '

'If you go away to the moon, my son, what will become of me?' she said humorously, her eyes gleaming as she looked up at us.

Aloo went back to his book and Mother to her sewing.

A little later I looked up and saw Mother deep in thought, brooding, and as she often did at such times she was picking her chin absent-mindedly. It was, I think, the first time I saw her as a person and not only as our mother. I thought of what she must be going through in her mind, what she had gone through in bringing us up. She had been thirty-three when Father died, and she had refused several offers of marriage because they would all have entailed one thing: sending us all to the 'boarding' – the orphanage. Pictures of her before his death showed her smiling and in full bloom: plump but not excessively fat, hair puffed fashionably, wearing high heels and make-up. There was one picture, posed at a studio, which Father had had touched up and enhanced, which now hung beside his. In it she stood against a black background, holding a book stylishly, the nylon pachedi painted a light green, the folds falling gracefully down, the borders decorated with sequins. I had never seen her like that. All I had seen of her was the stern face getting sterner with time as the lines set permanently and the hair thinned, the body turned squat, the voice thickened.

I recalled how Aloo and I would take turns sleeping with her at night on her big bed; how she would squeeze me in her chubby arms, drawing me up closer to her breast until I could hardly breathe – and I would control myself and hope she would soon release me and let me breathe.

She looked at me looking at her and said, not to me, 'Promise me . . . promise me that if I let you go, you will not marry a white woman.'

'Oh Mother, you know I won't!' said Aloo.

'And promise me that you will not smoke or drink.'

'You know I promise!' He was close to tears.

●

Aloo's first letter came a week after he left, from London where he'd stopped over to see a former classmate. It flowed over with excitement.

'How can I describe it,' he wrote, 'the sight from the plane ... mile upon mile of carefully tilled fields, the earth divided into neat green squares ... even the mountains are clean and civilised. And London ... Oh London! It seemed that it would never end ... blocks and blocks of houses, squares, parks, monuments ... could any city be larger? How many of our Dar es Salaams would fit here, in this one gorgeous city ...?'

A bird flapping its wings: Mr Velji nodding wisely in his chair, Mother staring into the distance.

ASSIA DJEBAR

The foreigner, sister of the foreign woman

'I know, I know,' Sirin murmured to herself, 'I know what I shall say aloud one day!' And she gazed at the circle of tiny tots, little sleepy-eyed boys and girls, who, for the moment, were her only audience.

She sighed. 'The Christian woman' some of her neighbours called her, under their breath it is true; they were still jealous, although Sirin and her younger sister Marya had converted to Islam when they arrived in Medina a little over five years ago. 'It seems more like five decades!' Sirin thought, as she got up to prepare the children's gruel.

It was always thus: when Marya left Sirin's house (Marya visited her sister once a week), the latter, overcome with nostalgia, hurriedly gathered together all her little flock – her eldest, four-year-old Abderahmane, the son whose birth entitled Sirin to the full status of a free woman, then the two little girls, born one after the other but quite dissimilar (the one fair-skinned, fair-haired, with huge eyes like her Aunt Marya, the other dark and sickly). Besides her own three, there were two other children, those of Sirin's co-wives.

These women avoided visiting 'the Christian woman'; when they met in the common courtyard, their conversation was limited to the minimum of exchanges. But they sent her their offspring as soon as these became a nuisance: they all knew that Sirin's spirits rose only when she had a swarm of children around her.

She would sit them down in a circle around her, like today, and whether they understood or not, she told them everything in a loud, almost ceremonious tone of voice, as if she were addressing an adult audience. 'Everything' for Sirin meant her life spent in Alexandria, her childhood memories of the glorious metropole . . . She relived, as she spoke, the festivities whose shimmerng colours still haunted her. The times when whole families, especially children, flocked into the streets, all in their holiday finery, and went in procession down to the river, accompanied by noisy bands of dancers. Some clambered on to boats, many others remained on the bank throughout this 'Night of the Bath' as this festivity was called . . . The Coptic words rose to Sirin's lips, and she recalled that they also called it the 'Feast of the Bright Lanterns'.

And the days when the children paraded around, carrying cakes with hardboiled eggs painted in vivid colours! Sirin saw herself as a little girl, the same age as her daughters who listened round-eyed; she saw herself carrying two eggs painted so magnificently that she had not wanted to break and eat them . . . To be able to keep such a multicoloured object for ever!

So many other luminous memories, images floating on a river of uninterrupted music (the clash of cymbals and roll of drums keeping time to youthful voices . . .). And always the streets of Alexandria, always the light of those long-drawn-out dawns or those bright-lit nights! The women around her sister and herself, with garlands in their hair, would exchange baskets of figs – those wonderful figs of Alexandria – and pomegranates. Dates were distributed to the poor in the cemeteries.

What good did it do to recall that profusion? How could any of the people here imagine so much wealth, save those who followed the caravans, save those of the migrant women who had lived for some years in Abyssinia . . .

•

When Sirin had finished telling her stories to her sleeping or passive audience, she began to sing in Coptic: she had a melodious voice that choked from time to time. She remembered the time when she was six and she was the one who had been singled out in that sanctuary – she could still picture its size, its grandeur, its dim religious light – was it yesterday? Seven priests, in their liturgical robes heavy with gold, one after the other lit the wick of an enormous candle, while a man (her sick father, she thought) had been carried in painfully to be anointed with the sacred oil, and Sirin sang and sang, as if her voice, as it rose up higher and ever higher, no longer belonged to her. Today she sings more softly that same hymn, which here in Medina becomes nostalgic, whereas back there, in Alexandria, it rang out triumphantly . . .

'If only Islam were thus clad in the voices of women and children,' she sighed, 'how my heart would have thrilled with belief, with an ardent passionate love! That would have helped me bridge the distance from the city of my childhood!'

The majority of the men here seemed so rough; and their wives were so suspicious, with only a confused idea of what she and Marya had left behind. Yet, Sirin recalled those last days, when they had been taken prisoner following the capture of their parents who were of Persian descent and had been sent God only knew where by the new Patriarch of Alexandria, the terrible Cyrus (Cyrus the Caucasian, El Mokaoukez, they called him here, with the respect due to a magnificent monarch) . . . and she remembered how, at the age of twelve, she and her sister had been led before him. He had looked them over with a tyrannical stare and decided that they should both be sent as a gift to Mohammed – together with a she-donkey and a mare bearing lengths of multicoloured linen! They travelled alone, accompanied by a eunuch and followed by Mohammed's ambassador, who had arrived from Medina with diplomatic correspondence. Their long journey lasted for weeks; they arrived at daybreak in this city surrounded with palm trees, which seemed to them little more than a village.

●

Shortly afterwards, Sirin had the good fortune to be given in marriage to the Prophet's favourite poet, Hassan ibn Thabit. For five years Hassan never seemed to suspect that Sirin for her part yearned only for songs. She would have been able to reproduce his own improvisations immediately, modulate them, amplify them, render them more tragic, more sorrowful, but Hassan never performed in front of her. What is more, he had once entered unexpectedly as she mixed a concoction of roots for some ointment or other with her back turned, and absent-mindedly warbled a song in her mother-tongue . . . To soothe untold hurts! Scarcely had she finished her lament than Hassan remarked sarcastically, 'I thought you had adopted Islam!'

'Is it contrary to Islam to speak the language of one's parents?'

He effected a retreat, but without appearing to excuse himself.

'No, to be sure,' he protested, 'if only you could speak Arabic without such a foreign accent!'

'The only thing which counts before God is my heart and its transparency!' she was about to retort, but she remained silent. After all, she was only a concubine, and she must not forget it. To be sure, now that Hassan called Sirin 'Oum Abderahmane' (mother of Abderahmane), he was so proud to find himself not only Mohammed's favourite poet but, thanks to his son, related to the Prophet's family. For Marya, Sirin's sister, had born Mohammed a son – a son who alas! had died at the age of two; but in spite of this untimely death, Abderahmane, the son of Hassan and Sirin, remained the cousin of Ibrahim, Mohammed's son!

More than all the literary honours heaped upon Hassan ibn Thabit during Mohammed's lifetime, he prided himself upon this unexpected relationship, which he could never have hoped for.

●

Henceforth Sirin spoke only in Arabic in the presence of her husband. Whence, no doubt, the irrepressible need she felt these last two or three years to recall, once she was alone – 'alone' that is to say with the children – that former time.

'Former', was far away, far from Medina, in the city of Alexandria, which she dreamed of every night now – sometimes the terrible eye of Cyrus reappeared, the Patriarch whom she had seen but once, but who had frozen her with terror. How peaceful the face of Mohammed had seemed to her, radiant and gentle, at the end of the caravan's long dusty journey, bearing gifts!

The nights were filled with visions of crowds flowing in wave after wave down to the wide river whose waters rose and gradually turned red – some claimed 'that the waters of the river turned to wine!' Laughter, songs, clash of cymbals, tiny children scattered here and there, dancing light-footed . . .

And every day at dawn, when Hassan prostrated himself in the dark hut for the first morning prayer, Sirin lingered abed, her ears still ringing with the festivities of Alexandria. Was she really still 'the

Christian woman'? Were her neighbours and rivals correct? Sirin doubted herself then. She forced herself to rise and set about her daily tasks as a mother: the only son to be woken, the little girls to be washed; the trifling gestures returned and Sirin emerged into a present of silence, of harsh sunlight, of dappled shadows in the cool courtyards. After the siesta, at least when it was not 'her turn' with Hassan, she became once more the children's story-teller, the melancholy, exiled singer.

●

Marya the Copt, whom all respectfully called Oum Ibrahim, used to visit Sirin every week, the day before Friday.

She arrived completely veiled (in a veil of very soft linen, a very rare shade of greenish-blue), her face hidden, her silhouette recognisable by its slender elegance. The eunuch walked before her, stooping, for he was growing old. Marya was accompanied by two serving women, one of whom was a young Negress, carrying packets containing surprise gifts for the children.

Then Sirin's co-wives made an effort to be civil, and their courtesy was almost genuine. The women gathered in the shady part of the little courtyard under a palm tree. One of the hostesses would very ostentatiously bring out from her room a silken cushion, another a silver tray, another a fan . . .

Marya would sit down with her customary simplicity, ready to listen to them all, lending an ear to the lively chatter of each of the women, replying to questions about her health, her welfare. Sirin, happy simply to see her young sister, enjoyed the admiring looks the children cast at the visitor. Lord, how beautiful Marya was still! More than beautiful, she was resplendent.

Sirin knew that once Marya had gone, the women of Medina would each recall everything said about 'the Copt wife of the Prophet': how, during his lifetime, he had always been under Marya's spell – the word was not too strong – from the moment she arrived. Her exceptionally fair complexion, the brightness which shone out from her eyes, the childlike roundness of her cheeks, her soft, curly hair, her delicate shy smile! Yes, as soon as Sirin went back to her room after Marya had left, these women would reminisce about the whole story: the bitter jealousy of some of the Prophet's wives in the face of the evident attraction Mohammed felt for Marya, jealousy that was all the more obvious in the case of Aïcha, 'the favourite'.

"The favourite", so they say,' Sirin muttered as she went about her daily tasks. 'I who saw how the Messenger behaved with my sister, I know that his favourite, the one who carried away his senses and his heart, was Marya . . .'

●

That, today, was just the beginning of Sirin's habitual monologue. Although they were entering the third year since the death of the Prophet, Sirin knew that she must keep silent on this matter of Marya's and Mohammed's union. 'Yes, I must say nothing for the moment,' Sirin thought: any indication that she might innocently let slip the truth of this matter, would offend the youngest, the most respected of the Widows. Respected also because she was a Caliph's daughter and the keeper of the Beloved's tomb . . . Sirin dreamed of this relationship of forces, her mind in a turmoil; she suffered from having no one to confide in. With Marya her sister, she never broached this subject, even when they were alone: as if, in the face of Marya's innocence, seeing her limpid, tear-filled eyes, Sirin was loath to cause any trouble.

So in the evenings after Oum Ibrahim's visits, even if Sirin foresaw the possibility of Hassan ibn Thabit entering her room, she began to hum her former songs. The little Abderahmane remained captive on her lap; he listened with strained features to this unintelligible language. He would recall it later, but differently.

Shortly afterwards, Sirin dared to declare to Abderahmane's father, 'I am sure that Abderahmane, my son, will also be a poet!'

'And his son will be one too,' Hassan replied. 'My father, who was the friend of Abdou el Mottalib, the grandfather of Mohammed, was already a poet!'

Sirin did not want to say that she saw Abderahmane as a poet, but differently: the child listened to her with feverish eyes when she sang for him alone. It would be those accents, Sirin was convinced, which would later give his verses a strange sonority; no, not just strange, foreign.

•

Twenty or more years later, Abderahmane, the son of Hassan ibn Thabit, was to report to Mondir ibn Abid, who was to report it to Osaïma ibn Zeid, who was to report it to Mohammed ibn Omar – and because the *isnad*, or Islamic chain, has been handed down thus exactly, it will be accepted by the most suspicious of traditionalists – so Abderahmane was to recall:

'My mother, Sirin told me one day: "While the little Ibraham, the Prophet's son, lay dying, Marya and I were in the room together with the Prophet (God rest his soul), at his son's bedside . . . My sister and I were weeping and moaning and Mohammed did not say one word to us. Ibrahim died. Then the Prophet asked us not to weep so loudly any more!"'

Sirin has become a mature woman; her son, a confirmed poet, listens to her; she is thinking of her sister Marya who died just six years after Mohammed.

Sirin recalls sadly, 'When Ibraham died, it was Fadl ibn Abbas, the Prophet's first cousin, who washed the little corpse. Mohammed remained seated, watching his son being washed, without showing his profound grief . . . No doubt his last, for alas! his own hour arrived just one year later! Next I saw Mohammed beside the grave that had been dug for his child, Abbas, his uncle, was at his side. The two young men, Fadl and Osaïma, the son of Zeid and Oum Aymann, climbed down into the grave. All, "people of his household".'

Sirin grew silent and mused while her son, Abderahmane, waited. He was accustomed to these sudden silences, as she dreamt of former times.

'You are still thinking to this day of Ibrahim's death?' he eventually asked – haunted as he himself was by the vision of this cousin whom he had never known, the Prophet's own son!

Then the voice of Sirin the Copt resumed in Arabic, soft, almost anonymous, like the voice of one of the hundreds of *rawiyates* of Medina, or the country around.

'That day there was an eclipse of the sun. Then the people said in consternation, 'It is for the death of Ibrahim, the son of our Prophet!' The Prophet, who had gone back into Marya's room to meditate, and to whom these words were reported, replied in vexation (I can still hear his tone of voice), "There is no eclipse of the sun either for the death or for the life of any human being, whoever he may be!"'

Sirin falls silent. It has been many a year since she had voiced her memories in the language of her parents . . . Sirin, Oum Abderahmane, and sister of the beautiful Oum Ibrahim.

Later, Sirin was to leave Medina, following her second son Mohammed, and accompanied by her eldest daughter Safya, to settle in Basra, in Iraq, where she died.

Traces of her descendants are to be found in this city. What is more, 'the House of Sirin' was to become a well-known spot in this prosperous city, at least until the year 150 of the Hegira, at the time of her great-grandchildren. 'The House of Sirin' then becomes a haven of peace, a place of protection for enslaved women, for terrified female servants, at a time when the opulence of the new society – composed equally of protected Christians, slaves and freemen of different races – causes inevitable injustices, internal violence.

One small incident – in the life of a pious personality, ibn 'Aun, who was married to one of Sirin's great-granddaughters – gives us a glimpse of some of the affection that Sirin the Copt left behind her: a serving-woman, working for ibn 'Aun, caused him to start up in shock when she presented him with 'a cooking-pot from which rose a strong smell of garlic'. He could barely contain his anger: the terrified girl fled to 'the House of Sirin'. A humble detail in a humble daily life . . .

Sirin lives on; her life, begun in Alexandria, was linked to Medina, as if, in the company of her beautiful, gentle sister Marya, she had travelled that far to witness Mohammed's few years of pure happiness . . . When, as the mother of the poet Abderahmane, the son of Hassan ibn Thabit, she has become a free woman, she finally leaves Medina, not to return to the place of her birth (although Egypt has become a Muslim province), but to travel still further East: to die in Basra, a permanent exile, protector of serving-women, of female slaves, of women with no support.

Translated from the French by Dorothy S. Blair

JAMAL MAHJOUB

Road block

The Storyteller drove a Toyota Hilux, red with a horn that played seven different tunes. Everything that wasn't chrome was painted a gaudy silver. In the back of the pickup he had red lights that spun like catherine wheels, and in the front he had a string of coloured fairy lights that were draped across the acrylic fur of the dashboard. The tailboards were covered in scrawled poems in Arabic lines; passages from the Koran where the word Allah appeared frequently. Though if Allah were in fact to cast his eye this way he might not have been too impressed with this storyteller.

His father of course was the original Storyteller. They still remember him in the small innumerable villages that cling to the sides of the Red Sea Hills and drop away into the Nubian Desert. Famous among the Beja tribes through which he used to travel on foot telling his tales in exchange for a square meal. One of the last greats, they refer to him, though most of those who might remember are either dead or have gone insane with age.

His son was a man who lived by his wits, a smuggler. He ran a ring of sizeable proportion importing whisky and almost anything else that you were willing to pay for. They operated out of the old port at Suakin, a ghost town.

•

It was after the curfew hour, the early hours of the morning in fact, when he came hurtling out of the darkness on a quiet stretch of road that would take him away from the coast. He was late because he had spent rather longer than he had expected with one of the girls at Mama Samina's. The narrow road stretched out in front of him and, despite the fact he was a little late, he was singing to himself in the cool dusty air of a December night.

The road block was a square shed of bare brick and a large mimosa tree. There were only two men there at one time. Bona sat with his rifle across his knees and tried to lean his chair back against the wall of the building. His partner had gone to bed complaining that his tapeworms were acting up and giving him pain. Bona hated his partner who was fat and smelled. They were from different ends of the country. Bona was an Azande from the far south, his partner was a northerner. As for any kind of tribal dislike between them, Bona was more bothered by the fact that his partner ate like a pig and smelt like one too. The sooner their spell here was up the better as far as he was concerned.

The lights from the Toyota were getting nearer. The Storyteller had forgotten about the road block as it was quite a recent addition. By the time he realised what it was he knew that he would already have been seen. It was easy enough to pull off the road and make a wide detour of the sentry post and rejoin the road later on. However, he didn't know the ground round here all that well and he didn't want to risk hitting a pothole or even getting hit by a stray bullet. His cargo of Scotch whisky was far too valuable to risk in some mad race in the dark. He slowed down and switched off his lights. With luck they would all be asleep.

Bona saw the lights go off and he stood up slowly. Cocking the old Lee Enfield over his shoulder so that it hung forwards across him, he rested his hand on the gun the way he had seen it in one of those Italian cowboy films. He stepped into the middle of the road and stood, legs akimbo, facing down the dark alleyway of the night.

The Storyteller saw the figure outlined in the darkness as he crawled slowly towards the checkpoint. Cursing under his breath, he switched on the sidelights and saw the tall thin man who was waving him to stop with a laconic flick of the wrist. He stopped when the plastic horns mounted on the radiator were almost touching the statue-like policeman.

Bona stepped aside and crooked the barrel of his gun at the figure in the driving seat. 'Out,' he indicated with his rifle.

As he climbed out, the Storyteller was cursing himself for his stupidity, thinking about where this man's partner was. He was wondering about what to offer as a bribe.

Bona was thinking about how the sharp leather of his boots cut into his bare feet. He was thinking about the way he looked, trying to remember if the rifle had been cleaned recently.

'Where are you going this time of night?'

'Home. I fell asleep in town but I have been working all day at the port.'

Bona glanced at the tarpaulin-covered shape in the back of the pickup.

'You've been working at the port today?'

The other man nodded. 'I work for the hospital.'

'Which hospital is that?' asked Bona carefully. He moved towards the back of the Toyota. The Storyteller reached for a cigarette, the bolt snapped back as Bona cocked the rifle.

'Just a cigarette,' said the other man, holding up the packet. Bona shook his head at the offer and waited while the Storyteller lit his. Placing the packet back in the pocket of his gjallabia, he rested a hand on his hip, inches away from the pistol that he kept under cover strapped to his waist. He smiled at the policeman.

'Which hospital?'

'The American Hospital, at Quaz Rajab. That's where I live.'

'I didn't know there was an American Hospital here.'

'Really? It's quite new, I suppose.'

Bona licked his gums, at the front where his two front teeth had been removed as a young man. He watched the driver very carefully as he sucked on his cigarette and exhaled, foreign cigarettes.

'And what is there here, things for the hospital?'

'Medicine.' He tapped his chest. 'For the sick, for coughs and chest infections.' Bona nodded understandingly. He stepped over and tugged at the cover, indicating it should be opened up. 'Let me see,' he said.

The Storyteller dropped his cigarette into the dust and moved across to untie the canvas cover, flipping it back so that the sentry could see the boxes. He held a hand out for Bona to inspect the contents. 'There you are.'

Bona stepped back and squinted in the bad light.

'Don't be vague,' he read slowly in English, 'ask for Haig.'

The Storyteller rested his hand back on the Browning automatic. He hadn't expectd the man to be able to read English – whoever heard of a stupid policeman being able to read English? He scratched his head.

Bona looked up at the driver. The Storyteller looked back at him.

'What does it mean?' He pointed with his hand. 'Don't be vague,' he read again.

The sentry stood back and waited. The Storyteller scratched his head with his one free hand. He looked at the boxes, then back at the skinny black southerner with the trousers that stopped halfway down his legs on their way to his boots, so that there were about six inches of exposed legs: two skinny bone legs the size of twigs.

The sentry shrugged and shifted the weight of his rifle. He was waiting. The Storyteller rubbed his neck. 'Don't be vague, ask for Haig?' he repeated. He spoke very little English and could hardly read what it said – he repeated the words the sentry had used.

'It means,' he said, 'that you should never let yourself become ill, and you must always drink your medicine.' He nodded enthusiastically, quite pleased at how convincing he sounded. Bona shifted his rifle again and sucked his gums for a moment.

'Let me see this wonderful medicine.'

'You want to see it? It's just cough medicine, brown liquid.'

Bona raised the barrel of his rifle until it was pointing squarely at the other man's chest. There was no way he could pull the pistol out faster than the sentry could shoot him dead; all he had to do was squeeze the trigger.

The Storyteller raised up his hands and showed his palms.

'No problem, officer,' he smiled. 'If you want to see, then you shall see. I shall open these boxes for you myself,' he continued, 'one by one,' he added dramatically, shaking a finger to emphasise his conviction.

Bona smiled and cocked his head to indicate that he could start opening boxes straight away. The Storyteller had no choice. He stepped forward now and pulled the canvas away with a jerk of his hand, his irritation showing for a brief moment. The sentry looked away and smiled inwardly to himself. The cardboard was slit and the box opened. Dozens of tiny miniatures gleamed in the starlight. With one hand on the trigger, Bona leaned over and plucked a bottle from the array. He held it up so the whisky glowed in the light. He twisted the cap off with his teeth and held the neck up to his nose.

'Cough medicine?' he asked again.

The Storyteller nodded resignedly. Bona tilted his neck back and poured the contents down his throat, draining the bottle in one go. He swallowed and licked his lips. Then he threw the empty bottle over his shoulder into the darkness. He cleared his throat.

'Cough medicine,' he nodded, and stepped back raising the rifle again.

This was the moment that the Storyteller had been trying to prepare himself for. He would have to shoot the man dead. He closed his finger round the butt of the pistol. Bona was talking again.

'All the same, are they? All the same kind of medicine?'

The Storyteller nodded, his finger finding the trigger.

'I'll have that one,' said Bona quickly.

'What?'

'That box there, I'll take that one.' He glanced back at the sentry post just to check if his partner had woken up, though he knew the pig would be asleep until midday tomorrow. 'Just lift it over the side and leave it in the dust.'

The Storyteller hesitated and then moved rapidly, pulling the case forward and over the tailboard. Bona nodded, then he waved a hand down the road and stepped away, lowering the rifle. The two men stood facing each other for a moment, then without saying a word the Storyteller pulled the canvas back in place and tied it down. He climbed into the cab and started the engine, punching it into gear and roaring away down the road into the welcome darkness. Above the racing engine and the howl of the wind past the open window of the car, he thought he could hear the sound of laughter. In the mirror he could just make out the figure of the sentry returning to his post with his prize under one arm.

The man they now called the Storyteller didn't really share the same gift as his father, but then that was what the pistol was for.

BEN OKRI

Converging city

When Agodi woke up in the morning it seemed that the spirit was still with him. Sunbeams came through the window and played on his face. The first flash of light he saw when he opened his eyes made him think of Saul's blinding. He remembered that he should pray.

He knelt by the bed in the single room and prayed through his mouth's staleness, but without his usual passion. He felt cheated of an audience. His wife had gone to the market where she sold garri. His two children were at school. When he finished his prayer he made his way over the disorder of empty sacks and blackened cooking utensils and fetched a cup of water from the earthenware pot. He washed out his mouth through the window while thinking about his financial crisis. He spat a mouthful of water down on to the street and the water fell on a girl who had just detached herself from the crowd. The girl stopped and immediately proceeded to abuse him. Her lips were painted red and she wore red earrings. Her high-heeled shoes made her legs look very thin. Agodi mimed an apology, but the girl was unappeased.

'God hammer your head,' she shouted up at him.

'Who? Me?'

'Yes, you, your very wretched self!' she said, relaxing into an impregnable posture of derision. 'It is you I am talking to, you who spits water down at people. You are a goat. You are not a man. You are a shameless fool with nothing better to do but spit water at people. You will die spitting.'

Benevolently, Agodi said: 'Is it because of a small thing like this that you're shouting, eh? If you have so many problems, I will pray for you . . .'

Interrupting, the girl said: 'Pray for your wretched self! I don't blame you. I blame your mother for allowing your father to touch her.'

Agodi was half-way through his invocation on her behalf when he heard the reference to his father. He stammered. Then thunderously he shouted: '*The devil block your anus.*'

And he tore downstairs after her.

He had rushed down one flight of stairs when he realised that all he had on was a wrapper. He stopped. He started to go back up. But the combination of sunlight on the filthy staircase and the magnitude of her insult aroused in him a peculiar humility. He decided to preach to her; there seemed no telling where a conversion might occur. He ran down the remaining flight of stairs and burst out into the street. Startled by the blasts of music pouring from the record shops, he soon found himself entangled in the hectic crowd.

He looked for the girl and saw her a little way up the road. She made furious insulting signs at him. He ran after her, shouting: 'You, this girl: the word of God is calling you today! I accept the sacrifice of your sinful life. You abuse my father, I pray for your mother. Why are you running? The word of God is calling you and you are running.'

The crowd cleared a path for him. The girl was already in full flight; she ran awkwardly in her high-heels. Agodi raged after her. Voices in the crowd asked if that was his wife fleeing from his insane desires or if she was a prostitute who had infected him with gonorrhoea. Agodi ignored the voices. Anxious to keep the girl in view, he pushed past a man who had been waddling along like a monstrous duck. Agodi's fingers were soon caught in the man's *agbada* sleeve.

'Are you mad?' The man asked, as he tripped Agodi with a wedged foot. Agodi fell, struggled back up, and found himself confronting a short man whose face was lit up with an expansive, demented smile. The man looked like an abnormally developed midget. He gathered the folds of his *agbada* on his shoulder and Agodi saw his glistening muscles and the veins bunched along his short arms.

'You want to fight?' the man asked with polite relish. He had incredible face marks. He looked as though he had been reluctantly rescued from a fire. Agodi backed away and looked regretfully at the girl, who was disappearing in the crowd.

'If you don't want to fight, then you must hapologise now.'

Agodi apologised in the name of the Almighty. Playing with his *agbada* and slowly flexing his muscles, the man said that he found the apology unsatisfactory. Spinning up the interest of the crowd, he said that the god he worshipped accepted only dog-meat as sacrifice. Agodi stammered. With great deliberation, for a few girls had appeared in their midst, the man asked Agodi to repeat his apology. Agodi didn't hear what the man said because he became aware of everyone spitting. He grew conscious of the smell of a rotting body. Sweating and confused, Agodi wondered if the smell came from his antagonist. Then he located the corpse of an upturned and bloated cow at the side of the road. Exulting flies formed a buzzing black cloud above the swollen body. Agodi had barely recovered from the surprise when the man tapped him twice on the head. Angered by the short man's audacity, Agodi held his fists before him. He hopped and goaded the man and at the same time made pleading insinuations about the fires of hell, the agony of sinners. The man found his cue. He made a strange noise and held Agodi in a curious grip and then tossed him into the air. When Agodi landed it was with a squelchy explosion as he scattered the flies and was immediately covered in a burst of foul-smelling liquids. Beyond the wild sounds, and the jubilant flies, he saw the world pointing at him. He pulled himself out, using the horn as a lever. When he had extricated himself from the belly of the cow he found his wrapper irredeemably soaked.

The city followed him as he shambled back to the house. A contingent of flies followed him as well. The children jeered at him. The man who had hurled him into shame was meanwhile busily distributing his business cards. His gestures were magnanimous and he had a disconcerting smile for everyone. His card read: COACH IN ACTION. PROFESSIONAL EX-WRESTLER. I OFFER PROTECTION OF PROPERTY, PETROL STATIONS, COMPOUNDS AND STREETS. AVAILABLE FOR ALL OPER-ATIONS. TRAINED ROUND THE WORLD. His name was Ajasco Atlas.

When he finished distributing the cards he shook hands with several people He told them that he had just come from India. They were impressed. The girls had gathered round him. He was seen leaving with them.

●

Agodi hid himself in the bathroom. He thought how every single person in the world had witnessed his shame. The news would certainly reach the Church of Eternal Hope. He was due to get a small loan from the church. He had been with them, as a faithful servant and crusader, for five years now. The Head Minister had explained how a church should also be a bank that keeps its members safe. The funds were controlled by a strict inner circle of elders. They gave out loans only in times of absolute need and on the strength of conduct glorifying the church. Agodi thought about all this while he washed the suppurating liquids from his body. Out of the corner of his eye, he saw a millipede crawling along the rotted plank wall. He saw three earthworms stretching their way through the wet sand that flowed out with the water. He blew his nose and his snot landed on the back of the millipede. He blamed himself severely for not having turned the other cheek; at the same time he knew that he wouldn't be alive now if he had. The ways of the world, he thought, were wickedly unjust. He dried himself and went back upstairs.

Agodi anointed himself with coconut oil. Then he lit three candles and a stick of incense and prayed for thirty minutes. The prayer consisted of one long sentence, breathlessly articulated. Wrestlng with the demons of language, he asked for peace and prosperity, he begged that the news of his disgrace should not reach the church, and he wished havoc on all his enemies.

When he finished with his prayer he felt sufficiently charged. He felt that he could now possess the day. He was almost sure that the city would concede what the fervour of his prayer had sanctioned. His body ached all over. He got dressed. He wore a thread-loose French suit which conferred on him a hint of suffering dignity.

He went downstairs to his little shop, which was situated in front of the house. It was a slanted wooden shed with rusted zinc roofing. It was painted blue and it had a padlock.

He sold items of clothing: shirts, trousers, Italian shoes and fabrics, sunshades and wigs. Most of the goods had been smuggled into the country with the collaboration of officials at the docks. His signboard read: J.J. AGODI AND SONS. GENERAL CONTRACTORS. IMPORTING AND EXPORTING. TRY US FOR SIZE. A TRIAL WILL CONVICT YOU. When Agodi went in he repossessed the spirit of the shed in prayer. It was stuffy inside. The available space had been shrunken with wooden chairs and unsold goods. Old newspapers, which he had never read, were in disarray about the floor. He didn't notice the letter that had been sent to him. He tried to open the window, but found that it had got stuck. He tried to force it open, but a splinter caught in his flesh. He banged his fist against the window, half-expecting the wooden frame to disintegrate. Nothing happened. He tried the window again and it opened without fuss.

He compiled his accounts for the week. He had made very little money. No one showed much interest in his goods. Enquiries were few, buyers were even fewer. He hoped that the small consignment at the wharf would change all that. He played around with his accounts as though, by applying some mathematical trick, he could effect a multiplication. His armpits became wet. The month's rent was over-due. There was a hunger in his calculations that made him aware of the city outside the shed. He heard the scrapings of a rat. A chafer fanned past his face. A lizard scuttled half-way up the wall. Agodi caught the lizard in a gaze and was surprised that it stared back at him. He looked for an object and was lost in the multiplicity of things which could come in handy. The lizard nodded. Agodi surreptitiously eased off a shoe, threw it, and missed by several feet. The lizard nodded. Agodi grabbed a handful of newspapers and before he threw them he discovered that the lizard had gone. Only its tail writhed on the floor.

He thought about his money problems. He looked at his watch. It had stopped. He shook it and it started ticking again. He gave it an hour. He put his shoe back on. It was time for him to go out into the city.

When he stood up he saw the letter on the floor. It was addressed to the owner of the shed. He opened it and the letter read: 'To the owners of dis shop, We are coming to rub you tonite. If you like call the police. Anytime is good for us.'

Agodi read the letter three times. He creaked his neck and twisted his head. There had always been stories of people receiving letters like this. He could not remember one person who was finally robbed. If thieves are going to pay you a visit, he thought, they don't write you a letter first. But he started to pray. His voice, quivering, turned into a complaint. And the sight of the lizard's tail made him see the city beyond: he saw people lying at street corners, scratching themselves; he saw the youths who grow angrier and then sooner or later turn to armed robbery; he saw those who are executed at the beach; and he saw the children who put a piece of wood into their mouths and die four days later, poisoned by their own innocent hunger. It all came to him in the form of shapeless waves of dizziness. He believed he had just witnessed a revelation. Again he thought of Saul. The real trouble was that he had not yet eaten. He swayed with a minor fit of vertigo. He surmounted the shapes by rallying the powers of the prophets, the Head Minister of his church, and Jesu Christi.

At that moment he might have collapsed if someone hadn't pushed open the door. Saved by the prospect of business and the immediate resolve to charge more than normal, Agodi was surprised that the man who had come in didn't have on a pair of trousers; and his underpants were in very bad condition. The man was very thin and his face was angular. His hair looked as if it had never been intended to be combed. He was so wretched that Agodi screamed. Then he dived for a spanner beneath the table. The man stood staring. Then Agodi flung the spanner, the man tore out of the shed. Agodi pursued him.

The man fled across the street. He ran, blindly flailing out against the heat and the noise and the dust. He crossed the full width of the street without being hit by a vehicle. He stopped. Puzzled, he ran back. He paused in the middle of the street and looked both ways. He saw nothing, except for an old woman cycling towards him. When he saw that there were no vehicles along one of the busiest streets in the world he laughed. He also laughed at Agodi, who had rushed out of the shed, brandishing the spanner, shouting that he had single-handedly routed the thieves of the city.

The man in the street revelled in his safety. He marvelled. He rolled over on his back. Cars and buses swerved round him. Drivers abused him. Motorcyclists missed him by the narrowest of inches. Then an intractable traffic jam resulted. Streets and main roads were blocked. Cars and lorries stood bumper to bumper. The whole traffic jam soon resembled a long and obscenely metallic millipede.

The Head of State was being driven home after a hectic morning at a trade conference, when his escorts found themselves trapped in the traffic jam. The soldiers and mobile policemen thrashed out in every direction. They kicked the metalwork of cars, pounced on lorry drivers, and beat up people who seemed to be obstructing the traffic in any visible or invisible way. The heat was a tonic and the official escorts were completely in their element.

But the Head of State was furious. He felt that the traffic jam was a particularly perverse way for his people to show how much they wanted him out of office. When he stared at the congestion all around him he experienced a sudden panic. He phoned through to Intelligence and demanded an immediate unwinding of the traffic jam by any means possible. When he looked up he saw, in the shape of an earthworm moving across the tinted window, the shadow of his executioner. Watching the earthworm out of the corner of his eye, he scribbled down notes about a new decree for the swift reduction of traffic jams.

Suddenly a shot was fired, which cracked the glass, and missed his head. He fell forward, a trained, if flaccid, soldier. He heard a further volley of shots. He had heard them every night for the past five years. He clutched the notes. He waited. He heard nothing. Minutes later he was told that he was out of danger. The plotters had been killed. Then the traffic jam eased, and vehicles started to move.

The Head of State decided to change his country. He wrote down a list of decrees to be discussed as soon as possible with the Supreme Military Council. He wrote down a very long list and soon ran out of paper. As the official vehicle eased back fully into motion, the Head of State looked over his jottings. Listening to the wailing sirens, he decided that the decrees were impractical and designed only to create martyrs. He had to think of his own safety as well as the entangled safety of his embezzlements. He knew that there would be even more attempts on his life if one word got out of his new efforts to clean up the stables. For the first time, he realised that he didn't really rule the country. He had no idea who did. Hot air blew at him from the shattered window and he tore up the notes with more energy than was necessary. When his motorcade turned into his barracks, when he saw the clean stretch of tree-lined road ahead, he immediately decided that the civilians had better return. Let them carry the cross of the country. He was going where the earthworms go.

•

The man in the street, who had started the traffic jam in the first place, attempted to get up. He was starving. He staggered and fell. People rushed over and picked him up. They dumped him at the side of the street. They asked him what was wrong with him and he said: sardines and Fanta. They left him in a hurry.

The man in the street lay there all through the day. He watched the dust rise. He watched the air saturate with smoke and he heard the desperate music that rode over the area. He saw arguments that led to fights. He saw the rich and how they created the poor. He saw the mice and how they fed on the poor. It amused him. He heard those with invisibly splayed feet, who were stalked all day and all night. He heard those that did the stalking. They were legion. He also heard Agodi start his Vespa and saw him ride out into the city. When Agodi was gone, the man in the street found the serenity to sleep. He nodded in his dreams.

•

As Agodi rode into the city he saw people at bus stops fighting to get on the buses: and he was glad that he had maintained his Vespa. At the Iddo garage he saw two women wrestling. They tore at one another's clothes till they were both nearly naked. Agodi parked. Soon many people gathered to watch the staged fight. Three soldiers circled the barricade beside the road. A man clambered on top of a trailer and delivered himself of a lengthy speech, which few people heard, on why destruction must fall on soldiers, thieves and prostitutes. He denounced the regime. He said fire was coming; and before he finished, one of the women was thrown. Suddenly the soldiers found that their money and identity cards had been stolen. They went berserk and cracked their new horsewhips on the gathered crowd. Agodi rejoiced that he was a man of God. And rode on.

Being a man of God didn't help him at the wharf. He had to sit in a hot outshed and wait for his contact man. He waited till he began to feel dizzy with the heat. Then he went out and got himself a snack and a soft drink. When he came back he found that his contact man had been impatiently waiting for him. The contact man told Agodi straight-away that his smuggled goods had been seized.

He said: 'My friend, the Inspector is very angry with what you offered. He says it's a mere pittance. Birdshit.'

Agodi stammered.

The contact man said: 'That's the way things go.'

Agodi knew what he had to do. But he tried conversation first. He told the contact man about the wonders of God; about how a man might be one thing one day, and the exact opposite the next. Agodi preached till sweat poured into his mouth.

The contact man was neither moved nor intimidated by God's reversals. He said: 'Save your saliva, my friend. Money na hand, back na ground.'

Agodi calculated that he could spare another fifty naira. He offered. The contact man took it as an insult. He walked away slowly. Agodi swallowed.

The man said: 'They will just burn your things for nothing. You can't be serious. If you are serious you will know what to say. You have the money, my friend.'

Agodi fought his tears. He pleaded. The man ignored him. Then Agodi tried to abase himself to the point where, out of shame and human feeling, the contact man just might relent. He listed his problems.

But the contact man's face was so unforgivingly impassive it might have been made of stone. He said: 'You are wasting my time. I didn't come here to listen to your problems. I have my own *wahala*, you hear? Either you want to collect or you don't want to collect. Which one you dey, eh? Tell me, make I hear.'

Agodi made promises. The man yawned. Agodi asked for a day's grace. The contact man chewed on the idea for almost a day before he finally consented. Agodi climbed on his Vespa, feeling that he had salvaged something from a really desperate situation.

He needed money. The church was completely out of it. He had not only slackened in attendance, but there was also the business of the cow. His wife was also out of it. He owed her too much money already. Every night, when she returned from the market, she looked more burnt and punished. Her eyes were now permanently red from the dust and pepper at the market. Her cheekbones stood out in relief and her spirit had hardened. She was definitely out of it. Besides, she was paying for the children's school uniforms.

Agodi rode around the city casting for ways of getting money to save his goods. He visited friends and relatives in their offices and in their homes. They were not particularly pleased to see him. They gave him food, but they had no money to lend him. He owed most of them enough as it was. Night fell and Agodi rode back home.

●

The man in the street had seen a whole day pass and had learnt nothing. He had settled himself near a gutter. He covered himself with unread newspapers. He lay down as if dead, though he jerked in delirium now and again. He watched Ajasco Atlas, who had gone past a few times, shouting about his feats in India. Ajasco Atlas had been intimidating people into accepting his business cards. He told everyone that he was an ex-world champion. He told them that he was a businessman as well. All-weather. He said he participated in the capture of two cities during the war and that he had done business with even the Head of State. All day he had warned people that if they were robbed it was entirely their own fault. He considered that he had done his best in offering cheap protection. Ajasco Atlas had, in fact, opened a small office along the street and was seen doing the most astonishing exercises in public.

The man in the street also watched the shed of J. J. Agodi with special zeal. He was the only person who saw the road move. He saw the henchmen of Ajasco Atlas move. Then he saw the shed as it moved gently. He saw it raised high as if lifted by a mighty and erratic hand. Then the shed disappeared into the darkness of the street.

●

Agodi rode into the compound and meticulously locked the Vespa. He thought about doing some very serious calculations. One hundred naira. The birds of the air feed, he thought. He had arrived at the conclusion that he would have to double his prices. He looked for his shed and he could not find it. The birds of the naira. He wandered around the compound, he went to the backyard. And still he couldn't find his shed. Saul's blindness. He called to his compound people, he called to the great wide world to come and see the extent of his suffering. Saul's one hundred naira. The world came and stared at the empty space where a battered little shed had once stood. They saw nothing except for the carcass of a lizard. They stared at the lizard and stared at Agodi. One by one they left.

Agodi sat out all night watching the space where the shed had been. He waited for his act of repossession. He abused the city. He grew hoarse. He gathered his wife and two chilren together. His wife was exhausted to the point of sleepwalking. He asked them to pray for the return of the shed. He started to cry and his wife severely rebuked him. The children cried and she joined them.

The man in the street, who nodded in his dreams, learned something. A very small thing. He learned where the earthworms go.

Agodi stayed up all night staring at the dead lizard. When dawn broke he fetched some holy water and poured the whole bottle on the lizard. Nothing happened. Agodi prayed and prayed. He felt the spirit leaving him. Then he called for kerosene and fire.

●

A week later Agodi rebuilt the shed. It did not have its former glory. He did not use it. Nobody wanted to rent it either. His consignment was sold off at the wharf. Then one morning his wife took the children and fled home to her village.

Agodi suddenly disappeared. Nobody saw him for a month. When Agodi reappeared he was seen wearing a purple-and-yellow robe. He had grown a reddish beard and his hair was in tiny braids. He announced that in the forests of the city he had achieved blindness and had seen God. He declared that he was now a true prophet. God and money, he said, were inseparable. He founded a new church and had several business cards printed. His new signboards sprang up along the busy street. Ajasco Atlas was sometimes seen around the premises. Everyone has problems.

•

While things improved, Agodi became aware of the man in the street, who had obsessively taken to watching him. Sometimes Agodi was sure that the man was making curious faces at him from across the street. And sometimes Agodi remembered the lizard that he had burned on that terrible morning. It had simply turned into air.

ADEWALE MAJA-PEARCE

The hotel

It was a town like all the other Northern towns he had passed, but it was uncomfortable in the train so when they pulled into the station he got off and found a hotel.

Behind a desk in the entrance of the hotel sat a woman. She looked up at him and smiled.

'Are you looking for a room?' she asked.

'Yes.'

'This way.'

She led him up some stairs and then along the dark corridor.

'You're lucky. There's a big conference tomorrow and all the rooms except this one are taken,' she said and unlocked the door. He entered and put down his bag. There was a table, a chair, a bed and nothing else.

'The toilet and bathroom are at the end of the corridor,' she said, and opened the window that overlooked the courtyard. A boy, about ten years old, was bouncing a ball against a wall.

'My son,' she said, and went over to the bed. She pulled the cover back and checked the sheets.

'I hope you will be comfortable here,' she said.

'I expect so,' he said.

'If you are hungry you will find an inexpensive eating-house half-way down the street on the left,' she said.

'Thank you,' he said, and she left.

He took off his shoes and lay down on the bed. Night fell. He switched on the light and took a book from his bag. He tried to read but the sentences made no sense. He decided to go out.

In the foyer he met the woman again. She looked up at him and smiled.

'I'm just going out for a stroll,' he said.

'Would you like to leave your key here?' she asked. He gave it to her and she hung it on a nail.

The moon had risen and the sky was littered with stars. The daytime heat had lifted, and a cool breeze blew from the desert. Here and there tall men in white robes hurried along. He walked aimlessly until he came to the edge of a cultivated field. He lit a cigarette but as he drew in his breath the smoke caught in his throat and he realised he had been weeping. He turned back to the hotel.

The woman was not in the foyer. He took his key from the nail and climbed the stairs. He lay on his bed a long while and heard male voices and then he fell asleep.

He woke with the dawn. His dreams had been vivid but all that remained with him were images that confused him. He listened to the others bustling about, shouting and laughing. So he waited for a long time until they finally left. Then he went for a shower and afterwards sat on the bed and thought about catching the train; but since he had broken the journey he lacked the energy to start all over again.

About ten o'clock the woman knocked on the door.

'I'm sorry to disturb you but I've come to clean the room,' she said.

'Okay,' he said.

'Will you be staying another night?' she asked.

'If that's all right,' he said.

'I hope you weren't disturbed last night. They made a lot of noise,' she said.

'No, I wasn't disturbed,' he said.

'They checked out this morning so you will be here on your own in peace,' she said.

He went for lunch. Then he went back to his room and remained there all day. In the evening he heard the sound of the ball bouncing off the wall. Later, he heard the woman call the boy in.

This went on for a week. Each day was exactly like the last.

One morning the woman said, as she walked into his room: 'If I can do anything to help you please don't hesitate to ask me,' and then, as though embarrassed, she looked away.

'There's nothing, but thank you,' he said.

'I would be happy if you would come and eat with us this evening,' she said.

He hesitated.

'It won't be much, just chicken and rice,' she said, still not looking at him.

'Thank you,' he said.

He waited until he heard her call the boy in, and then he went down. She had two rooms and an outside kitchen. The room they ate in was also the room she slept in, while the boy had the other room to himself.

After they had eaten she sent the boy to bed. They sat in silence until she asked:

'What brought you to our town?'

He shrugged and said: 'Chance.'

'How do you like it?' she asked.

'Not much,' he said.

'I don't like it either,' she said. 'It was my husband's town, that's how I came here, but since he died I've been reluctant to leave. This hotel gives me my livelihood although the responsibility is sometimes too much.'

'How long ago did he die?'

'Five years this December,' she said.

'I'm sorry,' he said. Once again they fell silent. Then she said:

'It's hard on the boy, without a father.'

'Yes,' he said, and then on an impulse he kissed her on her cheek. She put her arms round him and burst into tears.

Later, as they lay in bed, she said: 'It's not a bad way to live, running a hotel.'

'No,' he said.

'You can keep your own hours and between two people the work is nothing.'

In the morning he went up to his room and checked the timetable, and then he put his wallet in his pocket and went downstairs. The boy had left for school and the woman had cooked his breakfast. As he ate she spoke of the plans she had for redecorating the hotel. She quoted prices but he paid little attention.

At noon he told her that he was going out. She wanted to accompany him but he told her he wanted to be on his own.

Walking rapidly in the suffocating heat the dust got into his mouth and in his eyes. He got to the platform in time to hear the train approaching.

OKEY CHIGBO

The housegirl

Look, I don't want what I am going to tell you repeated anywhere. The last time I told anyone anything, that terrible gossip Nkechi Obiago got to hear it through God knows who, and now the whole world knows my life history. First of all, did I tell you that Madam has returned from Lagos? You should see the things she brought back. *Chineke!* Lagos na so so enjoyment! All kinds of beautiful trinkets that shone as if the sun and moon had come down to adorn Madam's portmanteau; all kinds of dazzling things from that wonderful heaven on earth where everyone wears the latest fashions and discards them in a week. She gave Obiageli a beautiful gown with enough wonderful colours to shame all the pretty flowers in our village of Aniugwu. Obiageli was ordered to give one of her old gowns to that witch Selina.

●

As usual, there was nothing for me. You know how it goes. Selina gets everything just because she is from Madam's hometown. My seniority as number one housegirl does not mean anything to Madam. The world knows how competent I am in cooking: Master is often asking for my delicious *egusi* soup, but does Madam care? The world knows how well I do the household chores, but does Madam care? Have you ever seen Selina sweep a room? It is as if her mother never taught her anything. I sometimes ask her who she is leaving the dust in the corners for. But that is another story.

●

Anyhow, you remember when Madam's son Callistus returned? It was about three months ago, I think. He was doing poorly in school at Enugu, so Master either pulled him out, or he got expelled for failing his exams. It is not that he does not have a head for books; it is just that he is such a wild boy, he never reads. Did you know he was running about with a harlot woman instead of reading his books? This harlot woman was also Chief M. A. Nwachukwu's girlfriend, the very same chief who fired a double-barrelled shotgun at a man he caught leaving his fifth wife's bedroom. You know the very chief I am talking about. Cally is lucky he did not get caught by Chief Nwachukwu. Obiageli says Cally must have been giving the harlot woman money because he was always broke. What a silly boy, eh? Can you imagine us 16-year-old housegirls giving our little wages to boys? Ha! We will make them give us money first.

•

Oby-girl says that he used to write Madam every week begging for money, telling all kinds of lies about new school uniforms and new books. She would send it because he is her favourite son. She is also making a lot of money as an Army contractor, but when I ask about my pay, she either ignores me or tries to bite my head off. Oh hard cruel world! Just because I ask for what is mine, she snaps at me. Do you know that since my father died, she has not paid me a penny? Oh hard cruel world! I have no one to defend my interests. Don't mind me, please. I will continue with the story as soon as I have wiped my tears.

•

Cally stayed home while his father decided what to do with him. I used to listen to him boast about the harlot woman when his friends came visiting. I would pretend to sweep the room next to his, and you know me, I would open my ears wide. You can trust me in these matters. If there is anything worth hearing in that house, I will hear it. The things those boys used to talk about. *Chineke!* Those boys are more rotten than overripe fruit with maggots in it.

•

One morning I found him sitting at the dining table resting his elbows on the table, and carrying his face in his palms. He looked like he alone had been given the task of shouldering all the world's troubles. When I asked what was wrong he did not reply. He just rose and walked away. I did not think too much about it, but went on to complete my morning duties by sweeping his room. Well, who did I find there but the headmistress of witches herself, Selina Okorie, doing the job. Or rather, she had stopped work by his table and was looking at something on it. I have to tell you that ever since Cally returned from Enugu, she had been trying to get into his good graces, running all kinds of errands for him, arranging his room for him whenever he messed it up, and always hanging around him to ask in her sweetest voice, 'Cally, is there anything you want? Can I wash your clothes? Can I prepare some *ugba* for you?' That kind of behaviour might have bothered some people, but it did not bother me because I am too big to be bothered by such things. But I am not surprised that Cally took no notice of her because her protruding teeth – which make her look like Agaba the dread spirit mask – are enough to frighten the stoutest heart.

•

I stood for some time at Cally's door, watching her, and she seemed to be reading something on the table. After a while I could not stand it any longer, and went in.

'SELINA OKORIE!' I shouted, and she leaped up in consternation, grabbed her broom and started to sweep rapidly. She slowed down when she saw me, then stopped. 'What are you looking at on that table?' I continued. 'I will tell Callistus. Thief! Idiot of no consequences!' As you can see, I am very good at insulting people in English. I did not complete elementary five for nothing.

•

'Your mother, idiot of no consequences,' she replied coolly. I tell you that girl can do things to drive someone mad. The blood immediately rushed to my head.

'What!' I cried. 'What did my mother do to you that you should bring her into this?'

'You insulted me first.'

'Yes, but I did not insult your mother.'

'Well, a light tap often buys a big slap.'

'You will get an even bigger slap from me then,' I shouted and flew at her.

●

Her *chi* must have been very alert that day, because she slipped through my grasp before I could box her ears shut, and escaped into the yard. I made sure that she was gone, then returned to complete the sweeping. As God is my witness, I did not intend to read what was lying on Cally's table. God knows I am not a sinful person, but if a letter is left carelessly open on a table, what is to prevent the devil from pushing an innocent girl like me in its direction? Of course, I first wrestled strenuously with the devil who clearly wanted me to read the letter, but you know how it goes.

I started to read the letter.

●

It was from his harlot woman in Enugu. She called him her 'dearest darling'. Ha! I am sure she has twenty other dearest darlings. The letter said that she was getting married to Chief M. A. Nwachukwu. *Chineke!* Money! Some people love it O! How can any woman leave a beautiful young boy like Cally for an old man like Chief M. A. Nwachukwu whose thing does not stand up any more? It's true! That's what Oby-girl said. And Oby should know, she has seen many . . . no, I did not say anything, I do not want to get into trouble. I am not like that terrible gossip Nkechi Obiago, who is full of more news than a radio.

•

Anyway, the harlot woman's letter said that she did not want Cally to see or contact her again 'in everyone's best interest'. Oho-o! I thought when I read it. So that is why he was so unhappy today. But it is good, I thought. It is not right for them to be together. Some women of nowadays, they have no shame. How can a 25-year-old *agaracha* be going with a 17-year-old boy, and be taking all his money? It is not right.

•

Later I passed him as he headed for his room and said, 'I know your entire history, your intimate and deepest secrets.'

'What do you mean?' he asked, looking at me suspiciously.

'Just be aware that I know everything about you,' I said. He frowned and looked into his room.

'Dearest darling,' I sang, and began to walk away quickly.

'Wha-what? What have you . . .' he shouted. 'Come here!' I scampered off, laughing like a hyena, and he charged after me, bellowing at the top of his voice, 'Comfort! Comfort, I will kill you for reading my letter!'

•

He caught me at the steps leading outside, pulled me to the ground and started to tickle my ribs. By now, I was laughing till tears ran down my cheeks while we rolled around on the ground. What are you looking at me like that for? Please wipe that sinful look off your face, it was all innocent fun. Your mind always goes to bad things. We rolled to a stop against a pair of legs in well-pressed trousers, and looked up. It was Master! Papa Callistus!

'Ah, I see you are getting along very well with the ladies, Cally,' he said, nodding his head very gravely. 'Just bear in mind if you get any of them pregnant, you will have to marry her.' I felt like asking him why he has not married Miss Onyejiekwe the teacher. Don't tell anyone, but do you know that the baby she had recently is said to be Master's? It is true! Nkechi told me.

•

A few days after this, Madam left for Lagos. The day before she left, I went into the parlour where she was with her friend Mama Moses the market woman. You know Mama Moses: she is big enough to fill a room and a parlour, so she occupied one couch all by herself. Madam on the other hand daily resembles the dry fish we use to make soup (I feel free to insult her because she is bad to me), and was seated in a small corner of the opposite chair. Madam is getting thinner every day despite her successful business, because her wooden heart is sucking up all the kindness in her body. Look at Mama Moses her friend – getting rounder every day even though she is not as successful, because she is so kind and good. Just the other day, she bought Nkechi a pair of 'higher heel' to wear to church. Can you imagine Madam doing that for any of *her* housegirls? All I can say is that if you are good, *Chineke* will reward you with the well-fed look of the wealthy, and if you are bad, *Chineke* will make you look hungry like the starving poor no matter how rich you are.

•

Anyway, that evening the two 'Business Madams' were discussing their business when I came in to pour the fourth bottle of stout for Mama Moses (that woman can take her drink better than any man in Aniugwu). Madam told her to drink as much as she wanted because business was going very well. Madam told Mama Moses that she was making the trip to Lagos to meet one Army major-general who would help her get a new contract that would give her bags and bags of money. When I heard this, my heart beat faster, and I solved some arithmetic in my head: if her business is working well, and she is expecting bags of money soon, then this is the time to ask her for some of my money. This is also the time to ask her of the promise she made to my father before he died. I don't know if I have told you this, but she promised to take me into her business and teach me how to become a big business madam like her. This is why I am still with her; I would have gone to work for someone else, but I do not want to remain a housegirl all my life. So that night, after Mama Moses left, I decided to ask about the money.

●

After seeing Ma Moses off, Madam went straight to her room to pack and make final preparations for the trip. I must confess that when the time came to go and ask her, my heart started beating poom-poom, poom-poom like that big drum young boys play during the New Yam feast. I walked past her room seven times, but could not make my heart strong enough to go in. I was about to abandon the idea when she suddenly called from inside the room: 'Who is there?'

●

My legs started to carry me away, but I forced them to stop. Why was I running? I asked myself. All I wanted was my money.

'It is me, Comfort.'
'What do you want?'
'I want to ask you for something.'
'Yes, go on.'
'It is about . . . well, you know how . . . do you remember . . .'
'WELL, WHAT IS IT? Hurry up, I have not finished packing yet.'
'It-it . . . Madam, it is about my money.'
'Is that why you are bothering me? GET OUT OF HERE!! Can't you find a better time to talk about it? Can't you see I am busy?'

●

I bolted out of the room, out of the house into the cool night air of the backyard, where I threw myself on the ground and began to weep. Cally found me there a short while later trying to compete with the heavy rains of last week.

'Comfort, what is the matter?' he cried, dropping to his knees and peering into my face.

'Nothing,' I replied, not wanting to tell him bad things about his mother.

'Stop crying and let us go back into the house,' he said, taking me by the hand. 'Won't you tell me what is wrong? Did Mama beat you?'

I felt like telling him because he is such a good-hearted person, and I knew he would sympathise with me, but I did not wish to talk at that time because I knew I would say bad things about his mother.

'I will tell you tomorrow,' I said as we trudged slowly back to the house.

●

All the servants got up at 4.30 the next morning to prepare for Madam's departure. Everything was hurry-hurry and quick-quick. You know how Madam is when she has something to do: she wants everybody to quick-march like soldiers. Romanus the driver drove her car out to wash it; Selina heated water for Madam's bath and then ironed her clothes; I fried *akara* and prepared hot *akamu* for breakfast. It was still very dark with the night insects still chirping, and the roosters just starting to crow, just around the time when spirits, both good and evil, abandon their wanderings abroad and return to their homes in the earth. Madam did not seem worried about meeting any spirits as she sat in the 'owner's corner' and Romanus drove the car out of the compound.

●

We watched the lights of the car disappear into the darkness on its way to that marvellous city where no one sleeps, then turned back into the house. I pretended to go to the kitchen to prepare the ingredients for the day's meals but as soon as I was sure no one was looking, I crept back to the parlour where I sleep, spread out my sleeping mat behind the long couch, wrapped myself snugly in my cover cloth and slipped into a comfortable and sweet sleep. This is why I am always happy when Madam travels – I can sleep a little longer and not have to wake up at 5.30. *Chineke* knows I am not a soldier man or a rooster that I should be waking up so early every day.

•

It seemed I had just fallen asleep when Madam returned to the house! She must have forgotten something, I thought, I must get up before she catches me sleeping. I tried to get up, but seemed glued to the mat, and she marched into the room and switched on the light.

'COMFORT!'

I leaped six feet into the air, shouting, 'Madam *biko-o*!' with my arm upraised to ward off the expected slap.

•

But when my eyes got used to the bright sunlight streaming in from the open window, there was only Selina cackling hysterically in the corner.

'Madam *biko-o*!' she mimicked between bursts of laughter. I tell you, it was too much to bear. I had to tell her a few good words.

'Selina Okorie,' I began.

'Yes, Madam Sleep,' she replied.

'Selina, do not insult me because I am your senior in everything, including age: 365 days is no joke, so please respect your elders. Remember it is me who shares out the meals now that Madam is out. If you do not look out, the meals that mice eat will be enormous compared to what I will give you.' She behaved herself after that for the rest of the day.

•

Later on that day, Cally called me into his room to ask why I was crying the night before. 'It is past now, don't worry about it,' I told him.

'Come on, tell me. It is Mama, isn't it? I know it is. You can tell me, I won't say anything to her.' I was silent.

'Tell me,' he insisted.

'Show me a picture of your har . . . your girlfriend, the one who is marrying Chief Nwachukwu.'

'Will you tell me what is wrong if I show you?'

'Yes.'

'Liar. You are more cunning than the tortoise of children's fables.'

'I promise, I will tell you after I see the pictures.'

He showed me a colour photograph of her. She is very beautiful with an oval-shaped face and a very fair complexion.

I said to him: 'She is very lovely, but I don't like the way she dresses. Why does she wear a skirt that is slit up to the waist, and a blouse that exposes all her breasts? She might as well just parade naked in front of everyone.' He laughed and made a playful grab at me which I easily evaded. I then told him that I had not been paid since my father died suddenly about a year ago. My father used to come at the end of every month to collect the money from Madam, ten naira a month, and he would give me three naira to spend. I used to be rich in those days. I could afford to buy earrings, bracelets, and chewing gum.

'How much does mother owe you now?' he asked.

'One hundred and fifty naira,' I replied, and he whistled.

'OK. I will see what I can do.'

'Just don't tell anyone I told you anything,' I said to him and turned to leave. 'By the way, I hope you have stopped crying over that girl. Do not worry about her, she is too *agaracha* for you, and all she wants is money. I am sure you will find many girls in Enugu who are nicer and more beautiful than she is. Look, I will cook your favourite dishes for you while Madam is away, and when I have time, I will come and sit with you and we shall tell stories. Very soon you will forget your *agaracha* friend.' He smiled and I left the room.

●

A few hours later, as I was passing the room, he pulled me inside and, to my great surprise, pressed a folded wad of notes into my hand. I uttered a short cry, and let it drop to the ground as if it were a red-hot piece of charcoal straight from the fire. He picked it up and gave it back to me. I counted thirty naira, and demanded to know where he got it, but he would not tell. I then told him I would not accept the money since I did not know where it came from, and he quickly said it was what remained of his pocket money.

•

I did not believe that story, but my heart was beating very fast as I stared at that money in my hand and my heart seemed to be saying, poom-poom, earrings, bracelets, poom-poom, earrings, bracelets . . . I solved the arithmetic in my head in this way: who knows where Cally got the money? He may have stolen it from his father's wallet, he may have broken into Madam's strong box, and he is so wild that boy, that he may even have friends who counterfeit money! But on the other hand, it may really be what is left of his pocket money. I will keep it for a while; if anyone reports missing thirty naira, I will give the money back to Cally, if not, I will spend it.

•

Unfortunately, I did not take the devil and his evil ways into account. He knows how to lead young girls astray just when they think they have the situation under control. The next day, Obiageli asked me to go to the market alone to buy ingredients for soup; usually I go with her or with Madam. I pleaded with her to come with me, but she wanted to go and visit a friend who she had not seen for a long time. So I had to go alone. The devil immediately entered my heart, and I tied up the thirty naira in the hem of my wrapper intending to take it to the market with me. 'If I leave it here, Selina might find it,' I reasoned.

•

After buying the okra and palm oil for the soup, I made a detour through the trinket stalls 'just to see what is available in case I find out I can keep the money'. It is not good for young housegirls like us to be without money for a long time, especially when there are so many nice things to buy, and other housegirls like Nkechi Obiago walk around in 'higher heel', and wear nice earrings. Lack of money makes us envious, and the bad ones among us may steal, while the others will spend foolishly whenever they get a little money. I left the stalls with only five naira left in the hem of my wrapper, and two pairs of imitation gold earrings.

●

If you know the devil and his cunning ways, you will realise that after you have done a bad thing as a result of his tempting, he runs away laughing, and the blindness with which he has covered your eyes is lifted so you can see the foolishness you have committed. It soon dawned on me that I could not show off my new treasures to the other housegirls and bask in their envious glances, because Selina would surely report it to Madam. I was gripped by a terrible fear: what if the money did not belong to Cally, and he had stolen it from Master or Madam? What if one of them found their money missing and called the police? Would Cally admit to the deed? I told myself that he was a good boy and he would, but what if they found out when he was not in town, gone off to school or somewhere? What would I do? Master or Madam would surely call the police. And they would send those policemen who don't wear uniforms and go around pretending to be ordinary people, those policemen who can just look at your face and know immediately that you stole money. I began to tremble with fear. I was ready to cry because I did not want to go to prison.

●

I walked into the house expecting someone to confront me and say: 'Comfort! Where is the thirty naira?' But nobody did; the house was quiet, and seemed empty until I saw Selina come out of Cally's room. 'You!' I shouted. 'Did I not tell you not to go to Cally's room, you sorceress?'

'I can go wherever I like,' she snapped defiantly. 'And where I go is none of your business.'

'Watch your tongue, or I will slap that devil out of your head.'

'Just try,' she replied, staring at me fiercely and cocking her fist.

●

I wanted to give her a few good slaps, but felt it was not a wise idea since I had not put away the earrings and they might be discovered in a struggle. Also at that moment, Cally poked his head out of his room, and said, 'What are you two fighting about? Comfort, leave her alone. I asked her to clean my room.'

* * *

I went to his room that night to tell him about the earrings. He laughed when I told him how I was unable to help myself when I saw them. He asked me to put them on, which I did, and stood admiring myself in front of the mirror on his table. You must promise never, never to tell anyone what I am going to tell you now. As I was watching myself in the mirror, he came up behind me and started to rub my stomach with his hands, and then worked his way up to my breasts. Yes, he actually touched them. He really is a wild animal, that Cally. I pleaded with him, 'Please, Cally, don't do that, it is wrong.' But he did not seem to hear. 'Cally, stop. It is a sin.' Eventually he stopped, and we stood around avoiding each other's eyes. It was the first time he had ever tried such a thing with me. I know that I am plump and have a full figure which makes all the houseboys try to steal looks when I bend to pick something from the ground, but I did not know that Cally looked at me that way.

* * *

After a long embarrassing silence, he put his hand in his pocket and took out ten naira.

'Take this,' he said.

'Why? What do you think I am?' I cried.

'Just take it. It is simply more of the money Mama owes you, so take it and don't be silly.'

'Don't be silly yourself! I won't take it!' I said angrily and left the room. But I took the money later. He followed me everywhere and eventually I had to take it. He made me take it. And if you really want to know (because your mind always wants to know bad things) we played the touching game again. Many times. I cannot tell you any more, but just remember that I am a good girl and I have my limits.

•

A short while before Madam's return, Cally was sent off to Owerri in Imo State where his uncle teaches at a secondary school. The man is Papa Cally's brother, and a very strict disciplinarian who does not spare the cane even on grown boys like Cally. That is why Papa Cally sent Cally there. If that uncle does not make Cally study his books, nothing in this world will.

•

After Madam's return and the big distribution of gifts (with none for me as I told you) everything seemed to return to normal until a few days ago. I was in the kitchen cooking, and Selina and Madam were in her room. It seems that Selina was rearranging her wrapper when some money fell out of it. The foolish girl had put it there and forgotten about it.

'Selina, where did you get this ten naira from?' Madam said sharply.

'My ten naira,' I thought when I heard her. 'That witch must have taken it from my box!' I crept closer to listen to what was going on.

'Selina, I asked you where you got this ten naira? Has the devil taken your tongue? You better answer before I slap it out of your mouth!'

'I found it lying on the road.'

'Liar!' (SLAP!) 'Liar!' (SLAP! SLAP!) 'I noticed that some money has been taken from my strong box. That's where you found it, isn't it? Speak!' (SLAP!) 'Speak, you ungrateful wretch that I rescued from poverty. Don't I send your mother money regularly? Why then do you steal from me?'

'Madam *biko-o*! Cally gave me the money, Cally gave it to me!'

'Yes, go ahead, blame it on Cally because he is not here. Why would Cally give you ten naira? You are a terrible liar and a thief! I am going to lock you up. Get into that room and stay there. There will be no food for you today, and I will send you back home tomorrow.'

•

My body trembled like someone suffering from malaria when I heard this. At first, I had thought, that witch Selina has stolen my money and now God is punishing her for taking what is not hers. But then, I started to solve some arithmetic in my head, and reasoned thus: if she took the money from my box, why did she not say so and get me into trouble? Maybe she was telling the truth. Maybe Cally did give her the money. I decided to go and see if the money was still in my box, but just as I left the kitchen, I heard Madam call, 'Comfort!' My heart skipped a beat and I replied, 'Madam *bi* . . . I am coming!' and ran to her rooom, my heart pounding.

•

'Stop cooking,' she said. 'Go over to Mama Moses' and bring back the yams she brought me back from Abakaliki. Go immediately so you can be back before the soup is ready. I will watch the soup while you are gone.' I dashed out of the house as fast as I could, heaving a sigh of relief. But on the way, my anxiety returned. Was it my money or not? Even if it wasn't, I could still get into trouble because it was now clear that the money Cally gave me was taken from Madam's strong box. Should I go and own up and save Selina? She is not really a bad girl; it is only envy that makes us enemies. But even if I tell Madam that Cally gave me money too, will she believe it? She does not like to believe anything bad about him, and would be more likely to believe that Selina and I stole the money and now want to blame it on Cally because he is not home. I could ask her to write to Cally to confirm that he gave us money. But then Madam will never do that, not for her housegirls. She can get new housegirls too easily. And besides, I was sure she was searching for a chance to get rid of me.

•

With these thoughts buzzing around my head like a swarm of big, dirty houseflies, I returned from Mama Moses' with the yams. When I got to the kitchen, Selina was sitting before the pot of soup, stirring it nonchalantly. 'You got out!' I gasped.

'Yes I did,' she replied. 'You thought I was done for, didn't you? Well, for your information, God does not allow good people like me to be punished for nothing.'

It turned out that Obiageli had returned from school to find Selina in 'detention', and had asked why. When Madam told her, she laughed, and said that Selina must be speaking the truth because Obiageli had caught Cally taking money from Madam's strong box when Madam was in Lagos. Selina was let out of the room with a strong warning never to take money from anyone in the household without knowing its source. No one was more relieved than me when I heard that. I found the ten naira untouched in my box, and promised myself to be very careful with it, and keep it secret from everyone in the house.

●

Everything now seems all right except for Selina. She seems to be crying a lot these days; her complexion is also getting fairer and her breasts seem to be getting bigger.

BA'BILA MUTIA

The miracle

Ba'mia waited anxiously for Reverend Father Tabi and his mother to come out of the church. Father Tabi had established it as a routine (after the second mass each Sunday) to come out and mix with the congregation. This particular morning Ba'mia was restless. He took hold of the sturdy ironwood stick with his two hands and hobbled to the school yard, away from the church.

As he pushed the stick to the ground, he hopped on his right leg and dragged his withered left leg after him. He had become so used to the movement that it was now a subconscious, almost acrobatic flow of motion which he executed without effort. The extra weight he exerted on his shoulders had left him with a broad chest and slightly exaggerated biceps and forearms. His thin waist, small stomach, and the baggy look of his left trouser leg, where his full left leg would have been, gave him a waspish appearance which was accentuated by his beady eyes and high cheekbones.

He stood behind the school and gazed down at the raffia palm trees and elephant grass. He knew his mother would be looking for him and, in her usual manner, getting anxious about where he was. He sat down on the grass. It was getting hot, but the grass was dry and comfortable. He placed the ironwood stick beside him and adjusted his withered left leg. A hawk was gliding in the air below him, rising and falling with the wind currents. His eyes tried to follow the stream as it meandered its way through the valley. Out here, alone, he felt at peace with himself.

Manyi looked around and wondered where Ba'mia was. A group of children was playing under the concrete water-tank at the corner of the mission maternity. Ba'mia was not with them. She looked further, towards the Reverend Father's residence. She saw Sister Mary-Jane walking to the mission guest house. The guest house was adjacent to the single-block elementary school. The local congregation stood in front of the old stone church in small groups. The men formed their own groups while the women laughed and chatted with each other. The locally dyed blouses the women wore, their wrappers, the men's handwoven shirts, and the children's *danshikis* looked very colourful. They blended with the hibiscus, marigold, and bougainvillaea to give the mission an atmosphere of heavenly beauty.

Father Tabi moved from one group to another. He shook hands, shared in a joke, listened intently to a family matter, as he moved among the faithful. Then he spotted Manyi.

'Ah, Manyi, where have you been? I was looking for you.'

'Good morning, Father,' Manyi said.

Father Tabi looked at her worried face. 'Is anything the matter?' he asked.

'Yes, Ba'mia,' she said. 'I can't find him. I saw him leave the church a short while ago. Father,' she added, 'I'm worried about him. Among the three children I have, he is the only one who's so remote and distant.'

'He's still a child,' Father Tabi explained. 'You worry too much about him. He'll grow out of it.'

'I don't know, Father,' Manyi said reflectively. 'He's almost fourteen years old. Everyone in the family loves him, but it's difficult not to sympathise with his condition.'

'Talking about his condition,' Father Tabi said, 'do you still intend to go to Menda? The Holy Father arrives in the country this week.'

'Yes, Father.' Her face lit up with devotional inspiration. 'Yes. We're lucky to have the Pope visit us at Eastertide.'

Father Tabi smiled. 'Indeed, we are. This is the third nation he's visiting on the continent. We expect him to celebrate Easter Sunday mass in Menda stadium.'

'Easter,' Manyi murmured. 'The Lord's resurrection. The time of miracles. Father,' she said, raising her voice, 'do you think Ba'mia could be healed?'

'Healed?'

'Yes. I want to take him to Menda. His leg could be made whole. It pains me to see him hobble around with that leg. I've always wanted to see him normal, like other children.'

Father Tabi remained silent.

'He can be cured, can't he?'

'It's a matter of faith and God's will,' Father Tabi said. 'You are his mother. If you feel strongly about it, then follow your heart's call. Have you discussed this with his father? You know he doesn't come to church – '

Before Manyi could answer, a boy's voice said, 'Good morning, Father.' They turned round. It was Ba'mia. No one had seen him hobble up to the front of the church.

'Ah, good morning, Ba-mia,' Father Tabi responded. He stretched his arm and shook hands with the boy.

'Where have you been?' Manyi asked him. 'I've been looking all over for you.'

'I'd better leave you two alone,' Father Tabi said. 'Ah, there's Sister Beatrice. I'll have a word with her.'

'Thank you so much, Father,' Manyi smiled.

'God bless you, Manyi.'

'Say goodbye to Father,' Manyi said to the boy.

'Goodbye, Father.' There was a trace of irritation in his voice.

'Goodbye, Ba'mia. Don't forget your catechism classes.'

After Father Tabi walked away, the boy turned to his mother. 'I'm hungry, Mother. Let's go home.'

She wanted to talk to other women and their families, but she changed her mind. She did not want to make the boy feel unwanted. His disability always softened her heart towards him. She waved at some of her friends as she began walking home with Ba'mia.

Gwan-Fumbat was waiting for Manyi when she came back from mass. His house was the only one built with cement blocks and roofed with aluminium sheets. The rest of the homesteads that made up the large Fumbat compound were a scattered cluster of mud-plastered houses roofed with long, dry, savannah grass.

Manyi, his third wife, the mother of his twins, was his favourite. He hoped she would be his last wife. He had married her because he wanted a male child, one who would inherit his name and sustain the unbroken line of the Fumbat lineage.

He had married the second wife because the first had given birth to three girls in succession. She too had three more girls. On his father's insistence, he married Manyi. Her maiden name was Kogah, until she bore the female twins, Nahgwa and Nahjela. Thereafter, she became Manyi, mother of twins and he Tanyi, father of twins. Twins were a sign of fertility in a woman. Perhaps the seeds of the male heir he was desperately searching for lay in Manyi's womb.

Gwan-Fumbat's father died at eighty-six, two years after the twins were born. Six months after he died, Manyi became pregnant. When she gave birth nine months later, Gwan-Fumbat knew his sacrifices on the family shrine and his repeated appeals for ancestral intervention had not been in vain. It was a baby boy. The long-awaited male heir to the Fumbat lineage had arrived.

But something was wrong. The baby's left leg appeared frail and unusually thin. Gwan-Fumbat's late father had a withered left leg when he was born. But he handled the disability with humour until a logging accident crushed the leg when he was still a young man. Not many people knew the truth about his one leg.

And now, Manyi's baby's left leg too appeared frail and lifeless. There was no trace of recognition on Gwan-Fumbat's face when he came to the Catholic mission maternity to see the baby. Despite the overwhelming evidence, he told himself that the baby's left leg was a temporary condition that would get better with time. He decided to defy tradition and wait for three months – instead of the traditional three weeks – before he would name the child.

Three months later, the visiting medical doctor from the city confirmed what Gwan-Fumbat already knew. The baby's leg had no circulation, no feeling. It was just a tiny bone and dead tissue. It was a dead leg. The condition was irreversible.

Only then did Gwan-Fumbat order the naming ceremony to be initiated. He paid the late-naming-ceremony penalty of two goats and a drum of palmoil. He knew it was his father who had returned. So he named the child Ba'mia, father has come back.

It was these thoughts that ran through his mind as the voices of the women and children coming back from mass reached him. He sent one of his older girls to call Manyi.

A few minutes later, Manyi entered his house. She bowed slightly and clapped her hands three times.

'Tanyi,' she said, 'greetings. I hear you want to see me. I just came back from church. I haven't started cooking.'

He acknowledged her greeting and motioned her to sit down on one of the several carved stools around the fireplace. He threw some splinters of wood in the glowing embers of the fire and fanned them with a piece of cardboard. A few flames caught the splinters and crackled into a bright fire. He added bigger pieces of wood and the big yellow flames lit the semi-dark room. He wore brown khaki shorts and a faded jumper. The light from the fire illuminated the face of a man in his late fifties. He had a broad forehead and bushy eyebrows that hung over deep-set eyes. The hair on his head was all grey, and the hands that threw the firewood in the fire were large and thick.

'I didn't call you here because I'm hungry,' he said. He poked the fire with a long piece of wood and stared meditatively at the flying sparks. Then he lifted his head from the flames. He looked at her intently. She was in her mid-forties, but her face did not betray her age. Her angular features, prominent cheekbones and firm breasts only added to her beauty.

He was not used to formalities, so he went straight to the point. 'Where's Ba'mia?' he demanded.

'Somewhere in the compound,' she said. 'Is anything wrong?'

He poked the fire again. The agitated flames lit his face. After a short silence, he raised up his head. 'What's this I hear about you taking Ba'mia to Menda?'

'What is it you want to know?' she retorted.

Her aggressiveness caught him off-guard. Then he laughed. It was a short, sarcastic bark. 'So you're now throwing my questions back at me?' he asked.

'Your question sounds like a riddle. Let me know what's in your mind, and I'll answer you accordingly.'

He laughed again. The laughter faded to a frown and a firm tightening of his lips. He began grinding his teeth. The diminishing flames produced dark shadows on his face.

'Ba'mia belongs to this compound,' he said emphatically, folding his fist into a tight knot. 'His place is here, with the ancestral shrine.'

A gust of wind came through the open door and stirred the fire. There were patches of light and shadows on Manyi's face. She stared defiantly at her husband.

'God has a purpose for him. He belongs to the church. The Holy Father arrives from Rome this week. He's celebrating Easter mass in Menda. This is a chance for Ba'mia to receive a cure – '

'He doesn't need a cure,' he cut in. 'He's not suffering from a disease. He was born that way.'

'He deserves to be normal, like other children.'

'If there's anything he deserves, it's our responsibility to help him accept his condition. It's his right to grow up into a man. Your motherly sympathy will not help him much.'

'You don't understand God's ways – '

'And let me tell you something else. Ba'mia's condition is his personal load he carries from the world of our ancestors.'

'What do you mean?'

'He's a reincarnation of his grandfather.' He ignored the mocking gentleness of her laughter. 'My father too had the same disability,' he carried on.

'But I thought he lost his leg in an accident.'

'He was born with a dead left leg. When Ba'mia was born, I knew my father had chosen to return to the family. His fate was decided before he was born. We can only help him accept it.'

'You have a right to your beliefs,' she said. 'He may be your father, but he's also my son. I feel what he suffers when he hops around on that leg. That's why I'm taking him to Menda.'

There was a tone of finality in her voice. The firewood in the fireplace had been totally consumed by the fire. Gwan-Fumbat poked the fireplace and looked at the hot coals that were left in the ashes. He looked around and saw some firewood. He thought of putting more wood on the dying coals to rekindle the flames, but he changed his mind. He looked up at Manyi.

'There's not much I can do to persuade you,' he said, 'but the truth is never hidden. When it's nightfall, when the day comes to an end, the fowls come home to roost. When Ba'mia grows up, he will know where he belongs.'

It was almost noon. Long rays of sunshine came in through cracks on the wall. They had replaced the light from the dead fire.

'It's almost midday,' Gwan-Fumbat told Manyi, 'and I'm getting hungry.'

Manyi stood up. She felt vindicated. As far as Ba'mia was concerned, she would always have her way. The boy could be Tanyi's reincarnated father; he could be the heir to the Fumbat lineage, but he was still her son.

'I know,' she said. 'I was about to cook come corn *fufu* when you called me.' She was almost at the door now. 'I'll send Nahjela to give you the food as soon as it's ready,' she said, as she stepped out of the door.

When she got to her house, Ba'mia was waiting for her. There was a defiant look on his face.

'What's the matter?' his mother asked him.

'You've been arguing with Father again, haven't you? About me as usual, I'm sure.'

'Everything I do or say is for your interest,' Manyi said.

'You've never given me a choice,' the boy protested. 'Don't I have a chance to talk for myself? Has Father or you ever thought I've got a mind of my own, that I know what's good for me, who I am?'

Manyi kept quiet for a moment. After a while she said, 'I'm sorry, Ba'mia, I never wanted to – '

'I don't want anyone to feel sorry for me,' he blurted. 'I can always take care of myself.' He turned round suddenly, gripped his stick, and hobbled out of the house.

The following Sunday Manyi and Ba'mia got up after the third cockcrow. She wore one of her colourful three-piece wrappers. Her son wore a golden embroidered *danshiki* over navy blue trousers. He also had his walking stick with him.

The first bus had already left before they reached the park. The second bus was full even before they got to the park. The third bus took a long while to be filled up. They did not leave the park till seven thirty.

By the time they arrived in Menda at eight o'clock, the streets were jammed with people. The most prominent sight was the variety of school uniforms worn by children all over the city. There were school bands everywhere. The police mounted roadblocks at every crossroad. They were checking people's identification papers. Ba'mia had been to Menda only four or five times, and he never ceased to be amazed at the novelty of things.

Both sides of the road from the stadium to the Catholic mission premises on the hilltop were already crammed with people. Some had been there as early as three in the morning to have a vantage place at the edge of the road.

Ba'mia and his mother were not so fortunate. They walked as far down towards the stadium as they could. The crowd was so thick that they could not go very far. They finally settled at the outskirts of the crowd, away from the main road itself where the Pope's motorcade would pass.

It was now past nine o'clock. The mass in the stadium had just started. They could hear the choirs from the big loudspeakers that were mounted in the stadium. They found a place and sat down to wait.

The open-air mass was over at eleven thirty. Ba'mia heard the shouts and yells of excitement from the thousands of people who were jammed in the small municipal stadium. He stood up and turned round to his mother. She was dozing.

'Nah Manyi,' he said, shaking her shoulder, 'the service in the stadium seems to be over.'

She stood up, craned her neck, and looked down the road. Small crowds were already trickling out of the stadium. Because of the big population most people had been unable to gain entrance into the stadium. But the throngs of believers lining the road seemed larger than the huge crowd in the stadium. They all waited patiently.

Ba'mia and his mother were pushed back ten or fifteen yards by the ever-increasing crowd. A policeman with a whistle on his lips lashed with a cowhide whip at the feet of the fortunate ones along the road. The crowd pretended to retreat, and the sea of heaving bodies undulated in human waves whose ripples reached Ba'mia and his mother at the back.

Without any warning, the stadium gates were flung open as the flamboyant motorcycle escorts emerged from the stadium. The escort riders were immaculately attired in white. They wore white uniforms, white boots, white goggles, white helmets and white gloves. They had not yet switched on their sirens, but their red lights were flashing. The Pope's walkabout in the stadium had not lasted as long as Ba'mia thought it would. Someone beside him had said they might have to wait for more than three hours under the hot sun.

Ba'mia used the support of his stick to elevate his head another inch or two. When he saw the black Mercedes emerge behind the escort riders, his heart fell. He turned to his mother.

'Father Tabi said the Pope usually walked around and shook hands with the Christians.' There was a note of disappointment in his voice.

'Have faith, my son,' his mother said. 'We didn't come here for nothing. God is on our side. I believe in miracles – '

The boy did not hear her last words. Even as she spoke, the black Mercedes suddenly came to a halt half-way down the road from the stadium. The Pope came down from the car and was quickly surrounded by aides and government security men. A bishop in a white robe also came out of the car. A slight gust of wind momentarily caught the Pope's white vestment. Instinctively, he reached for his head to keep the white skullcap from being blown away.

'Mother! Mother! Look! He has come out of the car. He's shaking hands with the crowd. Mother – '

'A miracle, my son. Faith. I told you. We must have faith.'

The Pope was just about fifty yards away. Ba'mia tried to think. The crowd in front of him was too thick. If he did not act fast, he would miss the chance of his lifetime. When his mother turned her head towards where he stood, the boy had vanished. Initially she panicked. Then she saw him about five yards away. It was his colourful *danshiki* that caught her eye.

'Ba'mia,' she shouted. 'Ba'mia. This way, not that way. The crowd is too thick over there.' The boy did not hear her. Her small voice was swallowed by the noisy cheers of the crowd.

Ba'mia began heaving and twisting his way through the dense jungle of human bodies. Where the crowd was too thick, he crept in between the legs of the adults. When he stood up again, the edge of the road was about three yards away. He raised himself on the toes of his good foot and managed to support his weight on the stick. He looked up, towards the stadium. The Pope was still walking down the road, stopping here and there, touching the foreheads and hands of the faithful, administering a silent blessing to those who reached out but could not touch him. He was now about thirty yards away.

Ba'mia made up his mind very quickly. He lowered his body and went down on all fours. There were only eight yards of legs and dust between him and the edge of the crowd. He gripped his stick tightly and began creeping forward. The smell of dirty shoes and feet, and the foul taste of raw dust in his throat and nostrils was becoming unbearable. It was suffocating. He thought he would faint. He could not go any further. He crept through the last pair of legs and, without warning, found himself at the edge of the road. He was standing in front of a short fat man who was focusing his camera on the approaching entourage.

'You dirty dusty cripple,' the man swore. 'Get out of my way before I kick you. Don't you see I want to take a picture?'

The boy apologised. It only infuriated the man. 'Get out of my way before I kick you back to the dust.'

Ba'mia moved out of the man's way and took two tentative steps towards the direction of the approaching entourage. He pushed his wooden stick firmly to the ground and raised his neck. Unconsciously he wrapped his paralysed left leg around the stick. He managed to maintain a precarious balance with his healthy right leg.

The Pope was now about twenty yards up the road. The crowd surged forward, yearning to touch his hand. He touched one hand after another, as many as he could. An old haggard woman struggled to catch his attention. Just when she was giving up, the Pope stretched out his right hand and touched her head. Her face broke into a smile and her mouth hung open revealing two rows of black toothless gums.

Some distance away, the motorcade was creeping down the road, keeping an anticipated distance behind the pontiff. He lifted a small baby girl from the arms of her mother and kissed her on the forehead. The child's face wrinkled into a frown and she began crying. He handed the baby back to her mother.

Ba'mia waited apprehensively. He felt his heart throbbing violently against his chest. The Pope was now only a few yards away. The boy held his breath and adjusted the stick to maintain his balance.

Then he jerked his body and darted forward. The police guards and plainclothes security men were completely taken by surprise. They tried to push the boy away. He ducked twice, feinted a fall, and slipped between their legs. He looked up, saw the Pope's flowing white vestment and grabbed it with his left hand. His right hand still clung to his stick. He could not afford to lose it. Two security officers fell on him and tried to pull him away. But he clung to the vestment with all his might.

The Pope raised his hand in a gesture of restraint. The guards and security men hesitated. They stood by in pensive anticipation, waiting for the slightest excuse to pounce on the boy. For a moment, everyone held his breath.

Ba'mia planted his stick firmly on the ground and raised himself upward. He was barely four and a half feet tall. He shifted his body weight to his right foot and, in a quick, sweeping and dramatic motion, took hold of the withered left leg and lifted it effortlessly with his left hand. A murmur of sympathy came from the onlookers.

The Pope laid his right hand on the boy's head and smiled. 'What's your name?' he asked in a thick heavy accent.

'Ba'mia,' the boy barely whispered. He was trying to stop his body from the sudden chills of trembling that had seized him. He coughed and cleared his throat. 'I want you to make me walk upright,' he demanded. His black eyes looked up at the broad face of the Pope.

'I will pray for you . . .' the Pope began to say.

'But . . . but,' the boy stammered, in a faltering voice. 'My mother said you are here for God. You speak with him. She said you will make me walk erect.'

There were visible signs of impatience on the faces in the crowd. The motorcade had now caught up with the entourage. The aides glanced at their watches anxiously. The escort riders were revving their engines.

'I speak for God,' the Pope said. 'I am only his voice, his messenger.'

Someone discreetly tapped the Holy Father on his right shoulder. He turned round and an aide whispered into his ear. He barely nodded. He turned round again and looked at the boy's dusty countenance.

There were tears in Ba'mia's eyes. 'I want to walk like other children. Tell God to make me walk properly. Help me with a miracle,' he said.

The black Mercedes pulled up a few feet away from the entourage.

'You are God's miracle,' the Pope responded, 'a miracle of His love and creation. You have to pray to Him.' In a wide, rehearsed gesture he made the sign of the cross over the boy's head. On a second thought, he reached into the pocket of his vestment and brought out a rosary. He handed it to the boy. 'Use this to pray to Holy Mary, mother of God. God will answer your prayers.' Ba'mia took the rosary and slipped it into his *danshiki* pocket.

Another aide came forward and whispered into the Pope's ear again. He moved forward and shook a few hands. When he turned round, television camera crews and a horde of newsmen closed in around him.

A uniformed attendant opened the rear door of the waiting Mercedes. The Pope looked at the waving crowd. He raised his hand in one final benediction.

'What shall I tell my mother?' Ba'mia heard himself shout above the din of the cheering crowd. His voice was swallowed up by the hum of the crowd and threatening throttle of the BMW motorcycles.

The Pontiff's face expanded to one last, memorable smile. Then he stepped into the waiting upholstery of the Mercedes' interior. The uniformed man closed the door mechanically. The motorcade began crawling past the main market, on its way to the Bishop's Residence in the Menda Catholic mission. The escort riders turned on their sirens and flashing lights.

The crowd had already begun breaking up. Ba'mia found himself swallowed up again in a whirlwind of legs, bodies and dust. He did not know when he lost his stick. He crept around in utter desperation and confusion, looking for it. When he located his mother, he was out of breath and exhausted. His face, arms and legs were covered with dust. He began to cough.

'What happened?' his mother asked him.

There were tears in his eyes. She lent him a hand and he stood up erect. His lips trembled. The dust in his lungs made him cough again.

'What happened?' Manyi asked again.

'Nothing,' he said between sobs, 'nothing.'

'Nothing?'

'Nothing happened. I lost my stick.'

'Did you . . . did you see him? Did he touch you?'

'The motorcade is gone,' the boy said, wiping away his tears. 'I'm tired. I want to go home.'

They began walking towards the old road that led to the motor vehicle park. She half-held, half-supported him. They walked in silence. A sudden impenetrable silence has descended on her and the boy. His face had a blank expression. It was as if he was no longer conscious of her presence beside him. He had retreated into an unfathomable world. She did not want to intrude in his private world, so she too kept quiet.

Finally, they reached the park. The minibus that plied the rough, dusty route between Menda and their village was almost full. The passengers paid their fare. The driver started the engine and the bus left the park.

Everyone in the bus was quiet. The monotonous drone of the bus engine was occasionally interrupted by the regular change of gears. Manyi could no longer bear the silence. She glanced at Ba'mia.

'What shall we tell Father Tabi?' she asked, in an effort to break the curtain of silence between her and her son.

'I don't know,' he said. 'And what about my father? What will you tell him?' His voice was flat, without feeling or emotion.

Manyi kept quiet. After a while she said, 'What are you thinking about?' There was a slight trace of desperation in her voice.

'My stick,' he said. 'I will need a new one.' After a while, he reached into his *danshiki* pocket and brought out the rosary. 'Here,' he said, handing it to her. 'You may keep it. The Pope gave it to me.'

'Why?' she asked. 'It's yours.'

He still held the rosary out to her. There was no expression on his face. Manyi took it reluctantly. The bus now began ascending the first of three steep hills before it arrived at the village.

'Tanyi will have to get me a new stick,' he reflected, after a few moments of silence.

'He's your father,' Manyi rebuked him sharply. 'You don't call him Tanyi. It's only the elders who call him Tanyi.'

'I am Ba'mia,' he said softly.

'What do you mean?' she asked.

'Tanyi's father,' he replied. 'I came back to be reborn in the family, to inherit what is rightfully mine – '

'Ba'mia! Don't say such things!' She recoiled back in shock and astonishment. She suddenly went pale. A kind of glow came over the boy's face. His thoughtful, reflective gaze had disappeared. It was replaced by a knowing one. He was radiating a strange aura that stunned his mother.

'I know who I am,' he continued. 'My place is with the ancestors. Tanyi will initiate me in the family shrine to commune with them. But first, he must carve me a new stick.'

Ba'mia did not hear his mother's reply. The driver changed gears and the bus jerked violently. Behind them a thick cloud of dust rose and died down as quickly as the bus's tyres churned it up. Ba'mia closed his eyes and lapsed again into another long silence, listening to the strained drone of the engine.

TIJAN M. SALLAH

Weaverdom

The weaverbirds, yellow feathers with black spots, so noisy is their ceremony. They congregate on the long, slender leaves of our palmtree, turning their necks and beaks in different directions. Their beaks curve into their feathers, fishing lice or ticks or just game. They peck the red palmnuts, which sometimes drop, and they would stare, marble-eyed, at the unfailing traction of gravity. The gaunt children in the yard run for the fallen nuts with fragmented rock pieces or slices of cement bricks, ready to crack the shells and nib the core.

The weavers are legendary birds, perhaps the griots of the bird-race. They have a penchant for intimidating noise, strident oratory, resembling a handful of chattering pirates boasting with their pranks and plunder. They squeak, regardless of the rhythm of time: dawn and dusk, crawling on palmleaves, or sometimes coaching their young under the apprenticeship of their wings. The weavers' small, acute beaks protrude in inverse proportion to the giant-sounds they make.

The weavers are great architects; their nests, intricately woven blades of dried grass, sticks, pebbles, leaves, and feathers, resemble dangling fragile gourds with openings at the handles, the regal thresholds into the weavers' bedrooms. Sometimes the crows and vultures vie with weavers for turf on the palmtree, but the drama resolves itself into the survival of the fattest; suddenly the weavers disperse haphazardly into the horizontal distances of the sky. Other times, the survival of the most numerous or of the most shrewd rules, and the larger birds yield for Weaverdom, envious of the power in sheer numbers.

The weavers have an English accent, punctuated nasal notes that grip everyone's attention. They have a habit of messing up everything in the name of Queen Victoria's glory, the Elizabethan successions, and the CommonWe or CommonWoe. Their droppings, hot and putrid, scatter on the yard, messing up the peace of the bahama grass, violets, mushrooms in their aboriginal wildness. Their droppings sometimes turn to manure, feeding the roots of gigantic baobabs, mangoes, and guavas. The trees sometimes pulse forth with chlorophyll, expanding uncontrollably from the weavers' excrements.

The weavers do not care where they build their nests; rumours have it that they came from a little island, somewhere in the northern ice, where the sun is for occasional rejoicing and where irreverence for weaver-ways raises hackles. The weavers do not care about the biological rhythms of others. They send their harbingers, and then flocks follow with fervent zeal, like a school of faithful Iranians executing their heaven-driven orders communicated through the sacred lips of the Ayatollah.

Song of the Grass

God pity the poor weaver,
That comes to us to teach us love.
His love of tea which is kin to us.
His love of ivory from our elephant's tusk.
His love of nests built from our flesh.
His love of gold from our sacred earth.
His love of god within himself.
His love of skunk within otherselves.
His love deep only as his beak,
God pity the poor weaver.

The weavers do not like grass songs, which they do not even call songs but chants. The grass is incapable of song and music, except after long and arduous tutoring by weavers. The weavers take pride in their elevated status, a pompous hubris propels their hearts, into nonappreciation for the earthly civilisations of the wingless. They burn the grass, forest and bush in the name of saving their souls from what weavers call 'heathen gods'. They force the grass to sing songs to their glory.

Song of the Forced Grass

Glory be to the weaver, the highest.
Glory be to his origins, the purest.

Glory be to his wisdom, the loftiest.
Glory be to his love, the finest.
Glory be to the weaver, the most glorious.

Sometimes the grasses resist, release their thorns like porcupines, directing their needle-line spines in defiance of weaver-authority. The weavers mercilessly set them aflame, ravaging entire grass-herds.

'I only wish,' says one blade of grass, 'that the rain comes and delivers us from such anguish.'

'Rain, rain,' replies a weaver, 'is such a treacherous player. An uncivilised bitch. A bloody fool. It knows no rules, except to salvage the green. It leaves us wet beneath our feathers. Rain, rain, such a treacherous player.'

Song of the Rain

Dear weaver, villain of anguish.
Let me anguish you with your own anguish,
So that you know there is more than a weaver,
A force that respects
The self-respect of others.

The weavers never like rainsongs, which they respectfully call hymns. Hymns threaten their sky-power, overwhelm their arrogance, engulf their feathers, soaking them with impotence. The rain comes in runnels of hope, embodying those essential forces that free the soul's eclipse in appetite, that free the gloomy body's inability to extricate itself from the Adam complex, that ancestral disobedience which accompanies the protuberance of belly-mothers, arousing their conscience. The weavers, so trapped in their self-worship and self-glory, despise the rain in the hub of their hearts. They prefer to die in the self-aggrandising sanctuary of their nests than face the truths of the rain.

The weavers see themselves as distinct birds; perhaps that adds to their over self-indulgence. Distinct in their tongue, which should rule the world. Distinct in their manners which would be etiquette for the world. Distinct in their customs and rules, which should be adhered to by the world. They ignore ancient Egypt with its pharaohs, pyramids, practical and mystical men; Timbuktu with its Sankore centre of learning; India with its spices, tea, and spiritual quests; China with its pottery and exquisite designs; Persia and Mesopotamia with their mystical wisdom and culture of the land; and Hellenic Greece with its Apollonian angst and Dionysian conviviality. But, weavers think, real history starts with them; before that, all is darkness. Or they say, history begins in Hellenic Greece and then into their island, and the whole world's history is the saga of their movements to teach the grass and other lesser entities of this hierarchical world about their enlightenment.

The weavers' mastery of the powder of death, which they ingeniously made from their faeces, gives them advantage over many other territorially myopic grass and shrubs. The grass and shrubs, rooted in place, never desire to sink their roots beyond their initial sproutings, albeit the weavers transplant them, and force them to sing this song.

Song of the Forced 'Lesser' Souls

God bless Weaverdom,
God save his majesty.
God bless Weaverdom.
God save her majesty.
God bless, God save
His and her majesty
Of Weaverdom.

Weavers love such songs, especially with grasses doffing their cap-like tassels and bowing, bare-headed, before the regalia of imperial Weaverdom. The weavers love to see the lesser entities celebrate Vampire Day (euphemistically called Empire Day). On Vampire Day, cannons boom; the grass, weeds, shrubs, lichens, march; the weavers' surrogates give rhetorical praise-speeches; the slavery of the grass is elevated as the sunflower of civilisation's triumph; and weavers in the most glorious isle of Weaverdom give praises to their inverted god in the Weavercan church, led by the archbishop of all arches.

Sermon of the Weaver

Our Father, exclusive to us the Chosen.
We your blessed Flock, blessed to take
Your lamp to the rest of the world.

By our means and any means,
To domesticate savages to be like us,
But never, never equal to us.
For we, weavers, belong
To your chosen weaver kingdom.

Our Father, who gave us the art of heaven,
Hallowed is our name, us great Weaverdom.
So that our kingdom spreads
Like it has over the isles.
Give us forever our heart and beak,
And forgive us for our exploits and extortions,
Like we forgive the savage grass
For resisting and murdering
Our precious brethren with
Heathen swords, machetes, clubs and bows.

Our Father, exclusive to us,
Lead us not into vengeance,
For we are too forgiving.
But deliver us from the spite
And envy of a million
Dancing naked savages.
Amen to our kingdom.
Power to our glory.

On Vampire Day, weavers repeat the sermon, loftily uplifting their narcissistic spirits.

All over the globe, weavers teach the grass, from the moment of initial sprouting to the descent of rust, that the world is created to serve Weaverdom. Their naked shrewdness, their procrustean logic and manners, and their arbitrary rankings of the lesser souls by their natural colours permeate the conscience of a passive world. Wood-weaver, Hunterweaver, Captainweaver, Pilotweaver, Missionary-weaver, Professorweaver, Reverendweaver, Soldierweaver, Parliamentarianweaver, in various ranks, recognised by medals, stripes, pins and badges, all journey forth into all global nooks and corners, sent by his and her royal harness, to discover those who long discovered themselves, to scatter weaver seeds, tend them with care and husband them to germination, to save the scarcity-syndrome and biting-cold of the weaver-isle from the envy and whims of cruel fortune.

And everywhere in Weaverdom, whoever comes nearest to aping the form and manners, whoever nature is 'kind' enough to bestow with weaver-features, is to rise on the rungs of the false-ladder imposed by imperial Weaverdom. The Indo-grass and Sino-lichens, the Mulatto-flowers and Arabo-shrubs, all in their confused sway to the wind of Weaverdom, swell their tassels with the weaver's arrogance, accepting the weaver's apex-status and pacifying and wooing their hearts with contentment for their place, which could sometimes pass for weaver and which gives them a notch over the Afro-grass. Even among the Afro-grass, the weavers cunningly ordained some with medals and honours like OWV (Order of the Weaver Vampire) and OSWV (Obedient Servant of the Weaver Vampire), titles which knighted them above themselves, turning them into Weaver-puns, errand boys with obfuscated integrities, catechists of self-denigration, imbibers of their own cultural suicide.

The weavers know the rain of self-dignity is against them; the grass and shrubs everywhere, seeing the coming New Earth, aim towards it, unrelenting in their pursuit of the Metamorphosis. The committed grass even strangles the weaver-puns, usurps the stolen manure they store in Swiss soils, humiliates them in popular grass-trials, and warns the weavers against their collaborative conspiracies against grass-existence.

KOJO LAING

Vacancy for the post of Jesus Christ

When the small quick lorry was being lowered from the skies, it was discovered that it had golden wood, and many seedless guavas for the hungry. As the lorry descended the many layers of cool air, the rich got ready to buy it, and the poor to resent it. The wise among the crowd below opened their mouths in wonder, and closed them only to eat. They ate looking up while the sceptical looked down. And so the lorry had chosen to come down to this town that shamed the city with its cleanliness. The wheels were already revolving and, when they shone, most of them claimed they were the mirrors of God. The lorry was quick but the descent was slow. So many wanted to touch it. A whole morning had passed leaving its dew behind long ago; and yet the lorry had not reached the earth. The wooden gold was easy with its birds landing and unlanding. And when the great gust of African rain came down, the wise still kept their eyes up, the poor huddled, and the rich shut their purses small. But nobody left. Come down, lorry of golden wood, with your cleanest exhaust ever seen, they said.

And the old woman was crying. They asked her whether she was crying for a wasted age, or she was crying for the coming lorry. 'Come and cleanse me, divine owner of this mammy truck, take my heart now, for I eat too much cassava to be good, I break too many proverbs.' They stared at her, then forgot her, for the lorry's golden rope had slackened, and was coming down a little faster. If only it could send down some sheabutter for the strained necks . . . and tell the birds to stop their singing so loud, for they wanted to hear the engine and place the range of its power. 'But we don't want material power, we want miracles, and the healing of the spirit.' The sceptical looked at the poor for the poor to share the slander of what had just been said. As if to say: when was material bread never needed? But the lorry did not mind the large curiosity below it. The songs of birds changed their direction small, and the seedless guavas rolled against each other. The soft touch came from the sky of fruit and love.

At first no one saw the gigantic message being lowered from the wheels of the lorry. The dancing and jumping of the children had continued under the intense afternoon sun. There were scores of darkglasses shined for greater shade. The message on the big card, having folded over after the sudden rain, opened out with the sun: VACANCY FOR THE POST OF JESUS CHRIST. The consternation among the crowd spread even at its different intensities: the sceptical felt vindicated, and snorted at the sky, saying that the eternal laws never favoured the wonder-prone, nor the innocent, and that if the heart was closed today, it would be closed tomorrow. And what was joy anyway, but a movement of brain energy. What a pity the African scientists were no different, they said! And the wise grew in stature in their own eyes, for the coming of mystery increased the questions and decreased the answers, thus leaving the space between for them to move confidently in. The poor waited and the rich wrote hundreds of cheques in advance. They were all preparing, preparing. And the old woman said as she grew in remembrance for them, 'Look at the shame of the children dancing when they should be kneeling, they don't train them to respect these days.'

Among the dotted neem tree copses, among the generous savanna beyond the city, the old gnarled palm tree refused its birds, the weight being too heavy for any more landing; and the rejected wings had risen and joined the golden birds on the descending machine. 'If we have birds going and joining the visitation, then we are in trouble,' whispered a brash young man with a girl on his hand and a cap on his head. 'You, Boy Kwaku, I knew you had no sense in that tangerine head of yours. Can't you read? The lorry is coming to advertise and then collect applications for the post of Jesus Christ from both black and white. We have never heard of anything like this and I can't even eat . . . but you, such new times will pass you over with nothing showing in you!' screamed an old man with his beard woven round to the back of his head. The old man looked with scorn at the old woman of remembrance, wondering when she was going to be prophetic again between the mouthfuls of roasted cocoyam. Boy Kwaku laughed to his adoring girl, but the old man ignored him, and patted his black beard in the sun.

Even in this time of upward eyes you couldn't understand why the sun and the rain changed places so often. You ate atua out of season in the rain, and sho in season in the sun. And the shades were stolen rests from the hot valleys. Turn your eyes sideways, you crowd! For the golden lorry with its divine vacancy was getting bigger as it descended. 'It is coming to kill us!' shouted a little girl running from one shade to another. Dogs, sheep, goats, and hens moved about with a curious stiffness, kokrokoo. 'Daddy, buy the lorry for me, Daddy, buy the lorry for me now now now! . . .'

It wasn't long before the priests, and the policemen came: for the simple reason that rumours had grown that there was a deep-bronze man in the golden lorry. 'We can talk to something we can touch then,' enthused the two groups. Before the priests came they had insisted that half the town fill the churches, since if this was a divine presence, it would certainly visit a church first. Furthermore, if the sons and daughters of men were to believe in the big VACANCY sign flapping above the valleys, then surely the search indicated would be in a church. But Bishop Bawa asked Father Vea, 'Is there anything in the gospels that speaks of a vacancy for the Son of God?' Father Vea, a man that followed his own ways, had entered the valleys with a huge karate jump that he had been trying to teach the bishop to do. These unusual clerics had arrived before the usual ones, and they had also arrived before the herbalists and the traditional priests. 'My Lord, we are in unusual times . . . and I love it!' There was a loud but shortlived cheer for the jump. But the wise were sarcastic about these visitational acrobatics.

True, there was a dark bronze man with very clear eyes at the wheel of the lorry. The murmuring in the crowd grew, as the untidy but immaculate-eyed man of ropegold presented one expressionless look after another. The old rain came back and wet the lorry. But the crowd remained dry. Father Vea was jumping about and praying at the same time, as the lone traditional priest, now come, poured libation at great speed. He was trying to beat the golden lorry to Asaase Yaa before it landed. The cries of goats were stuck in the mouth, and Father Vea was going round the mouths of goats trying hard to unstick the sounds.

He shouted, 'The more apocalyptic we appear, the easier it would be for the divine to pass us by! Let the goats be normal!' 'Go back to your African Gonja karate, Father!' someone shouted back. At the edges of the small ponds the guinea grass was motionless with the cries of doves. Bishop Bawa had been told of what was happening while he was in his vast rice and pepper farms. He had been strolling up and down just behind his open-air raffia altar. He and Father Vea had jumped in surprise together, but Father Vea had jumped higher.

And then the lorry of wooden gold began to shake violently as it prepared to land. The expression of the bronze lorry man had now changed to one of intense concentration. The police moved back, their weapons unconsciously at the ready. Oddly enough, the crowd surged forward instead of back. Father Vea held his hands high in an unknowing triumph . . .

So unknowing that the speed of the bronze man was not even witnessed as he raised a thick arm and gave Father Vea a massive blow on the neck. Before Vea fell, the bronze-black giant had already collected the rifles of the police, with the same lightning speed, and all this done without leaving the lorry. And long before the army's three armoured vehicles could move the bronze man had already neutralised their wheels and guns. The old woman of remembrance was sobbing and tending Father Vea. The poor were ready for any old order to be broken, while the rich were inching slowly away, their chequebooks hidden: how could you buy a truck with such a violent driver masquerading as the keeper of the vacancy of Jesus Christ? 'Didn't I tell you he was coming to kill us?' shouted the little girl again, with all her shades finished. The cheque keepers must be sobbing, thought the bearded old man.

The quick African dusk had come as the bronze man finally jumped out of the woodgold. He stood there staring at the earth, with utter concentration. The heavens were dragging away the last of the red sunset, and the ropegold hung uselessly out of the sky. The crowd couldn't bear the man's concentration as small branches caught fire, and birds flew away from smoke.

'I fear nothing!' shouted the dark bronze man suddenly. 'I am the master of the skies, and I am the one that killed Jesus Christ behind the millionth galaxy of stars. I have come to seek a replacement for the

Lord, because the galaxies have never been the same since his death. I am a violent man looking for peace.' Bishop Bawa looked with more scorn than pity at the strong skytraveller towering above the rest of them. The sceptical looked with dismay at what was happening: they wanted clarity rather than mystery. The wise threw out different questions: 'If you have killed the Lord, why should you be allowed to seek a replacement?'

'You have given me the chance to forgive you,' mumbled Father Vea, trying to rise to his feet under the hands of the forgotten woman of remembrance. Biship Bawa beckoned to Vea to continue to rest, as he himself moved forward to speak, his rice and pepper farms echoing in his head: he always felt nearer to God through mundane physical images, seen in crises. 'If you have killed Jesus,' asserted the little girl of shades, 'then this is the town where you too will die.' The animals scattered as the skytraveller combed dust out of his thick hair. The wise wanted miracles to liberate their wisdom ... but miracles on whose behalf? 'Shame to the sky of murder!' someone shouted against the hard forehead of the bronzling. The first sky of descending love had changed to this. There were now brusque orders and there was violence. But Bishop Bawa spoke all the same, 'Did you kill the Lord's soul or did you kill his body?' The bronzling snorted at the bishop, but answered, 'Show me the three most important places of the neighbouring city, and I will tell you the secret of Jesus Christ.'

'I will show you five places, one here and four in the city; if only you would do two important things: kill me in the same way you killed the Lord, but before this you will tell me all about the lorry of wooden gold,' said Father Vea with conviction, struggling on to his feet. The traditional priest had appeared on the hills watching everything in the valleys. And without warning, with the dusk dead to the evening, the hard traveller crushed a dog's head with his foot to signify the agreement. 'Shame to your violence!' the traditional priest shouted down. The traveller looked to the hills with contempt and slept there standing up.

The dawn couldn't catch the traveller, for he had already left with Father Vea towards the city. Bishop Bawa and the traditional priest had already gathered the crowd, and they had all sworn to prepare for the giant's destruction, this killer of eternity. They had decided to take the lorry of wooden gold, to get it to help them. Surely anything golden was good . . . 'This lorry is no better than its master, I tell you sharp,' warned the little girl.

There was a threat, even damnation, in the air on the road to the city. Father Vea had tried kicks, chops and trips in surprise on the skytraveller, but the strength of the latter was incredible. These attempts only angered the bronzling, thus creating a mood of ruthlessness that did not seem to belong here on earth. When this giant urinated he created a stream that went on for ever. Vea soldiered on, tripping and panting and rebelling simultaneously in front of the wooden gold man. The sun had given the city a yellow look.

'You evil African bronze man, I will show you the mortuary, the seat of government, the courtroom, and the historical room. The fifth place will be the church of the shrine back in the town. I hope you survive this,' Father said to the bronzeman, who had taken on that intense concentration again . . . as if he were expecting something. 'Sometimes I feel the spirit of the Lord, so the sooner I replace the body of the dead Jesus the clearer my mind will be . . . I have enemies from other galaxies. I am the first evil galactic African bronzeman; and before I arrive at simpler places like the earth, I send false images of beauty and peace before me by a secret process of osmosis . . .' 'Why are you filling me fat with all this information before you kill me in the same way you killed Jesus . . .?' complained Father Vea with no trace of fear. The bronzeman continued regardless, with the birds back at his head, 'My lorry of wooden gold has its own mind, created through a new type of computer. Back in the galaxies we call the Lord The Spiriter!' He laughed a deep pre-set laugh at his own words. But Father Vea stumbled on in thought, his legs bleeding from the scratching of ivy bush-green and blackberry. 'We will go to the mortuary first, but we need permission . . .' Vea said. 'I will break the doors down even from a distance,' was the curt reply from bronze mouth.

Father Vea stopped running before the giant strides of the giantman, and asked, 'Why is the mortuary one of the three places you want to see? How can the dead apply for the post of a Jesus here . . .' Giantman wasn't paying attention, and had rather taken on his sudden concentration. He boomed out, 'There are two tanks hidden near the doorway . . .' And the tanks' cannons fired at once, the bombs bouncing off his chest almost as if they were small stones. He gave out his huge laughter as he broke the mortuary door down, saying, 'Sometimes the better people are dead. If I find someone suitable to fill the vacancy, I'll take him back and resurrect him through deep ice plus the manipulation of time . . .' He was still laughing as he crushed the tracks of the tanks and walked into the house of the dead, with the officials and attendants scattering in fear. 'Wouldn't you like to meet any literary men?' Father Vea ventured, with the giant laughter still in progress, and Vea regretting his intuition that he should have learnt a better karate since no one anticipated an invincible man.

The atmosphere had changed with the afternoon yellowing through the opaque windows. Father Vea had not been able to get a word from bronzeman as the latter, callous and casual, went among the dead both frozen and unfrozen, on the postmortem tables and off them. Vea was shaking with uncontrollable anger as the dead were desecrated, and had tried his useless karate kicks again. He said a quick formal prayer and then bellowed to the giantman, as if in a trance, 'Leave that cool face alone, the poor man died only last week from a broken heart and diabetes, since his children had become ashamed of his old face, his stammer, and his poverty; and the last straw was when his eldest daughter got married without his knowledge. His wife had been helping this filial hate along . . . and that woman had died in an accident. Are you allowing women applying to be Jesus, if not please leave her alone! Judging these lives is incidental to you, and I am telling their lives out of the need to defend them from you. I know you think I'm giving you information, how stupid!' The blow that Father Vea received knocked him out altogether.

Father Vea woke to these words from his adversary. 'I have selected two potential candidates. They are on the floor at the moment. Carry them into the golden lorry outside. I called it here.' Vea caught himself doing exactly as he was told. This obedience was what he would have to fight against, voluntary and involuntary slavery. Yet one part of his mind remained free and full of disjointed prayers. The birds were no longer around the wooden gold lorry, and its guavas of bribery were rotten. 'But one of them is a woman,' exclaimed Vea, knowing full well that he could get the answer that the new Jesus-to-be could be a woman. He received no answer as the lorrygold drove off by itself to put the bodies where it first landed, the valley now deserted except for the echoing sounds of intense activity in the churches and the shrines. Only the same little girl stood by her finished shades.

'There is a joy in using an ancestral laser gun, arrived at from centuries of experiments sustained by gari, herbs, bones and metal. The galaxies are very ancestral, hence the killing and the search for the Lord. If there's no spirit beyond the gadgets then the gadgets take over . . .' said the giantman with a silly smile on his face, pushing Father Vea brutally towards the next place of visit: the courtrooms. 'I believe this spirit can be evil as well as good,' panted Vea, trying to correct the hate in his heart for this galactic man with his prestidigitatory mammy truck. 'The means always justifies the end in the galaxies,' shouted giantman, now not only smiling but laughing between the pushing of the priest. Vea stopped abruptly, and then said as he was prodded forward again, 'I see you don't have real intelligence up there . . .'

Bronzeman's laughter went from the mortuary right into the court-rooms, where the yellow atmosphere continued through the fan and the floor of ochre terrazzo. The afternoon was old. But the laughter continued to be new as it pierced through the back of Father Vea. And what was strange about the court was that the judge and everyone else behaved as if the giantman and the Father hadn't entered at all. The case under trial continued through the presence of the man of the galaxies. 'I am used to attention,' he roared, raising his hands so that they almost touched the high court ceiling. 'I get attention among the planets, and I demand it here as of right.' The lawyers continued to argue their cases, and the witnesses came. Father Vea, now totally exhausted, was sitting staring on the court floor. 'I have come here to fill the vacancy for the post of Jesus Christ, and I will take by force anyone I consider a suitable candidate . . .'

'My lord, I believe the learned counsel has misread the point I am trying to make in connection with the third witness for the defence . . .' The court continued to ignore the giantman as Father Vea, regaining his breath, at last looked around in amazement.

To the surprise and enragement of the man of wooden gold, the judge started to speak directly to him. 'I am happy that you as the accused have now been apprehended, but I demand that you comport yourself properly in court. I may have to hold you in contempt. We in this city have been waiting for centuries to put you on trial for your criminal destruction of the spirit in space, of which the killing of the son of the Master of the universe is the biggest symbol. We are not afraid of your brutal power. The trial will continue whether you kill us all together or one by one.' There was complete silence as Bishop Bawa walked into the court and stood defiantly below the judge. He had pepper in one hand and rice in the other. He said to the hard-faced wooden golding, 'After you have finished in the courtrooms, the governing rooms and the churches and shrines, we will be waiting for you in the historical rooms . . . where we assure you that you will get all the candidates you need for the vacancy of the Lord.' The giantman killed a bailiff with one blow, shouting, 'Show me the governing places, my patience is wearing thin!' And in his own mind he had only left the life of the judge intact because he could be a live candidate for the astral vacancy. Giantman had not forgotten Father Vea: he pulled him along, as Bishop Bawa rushed back towards the town, with a grim look on his face.

At first the cabinet rooms smelt of the same old politics: the half-truth, the slant, the cynical, the secret, the sabotage, the murder, the brazen, the corrupt, the thievery, the apathy, the sycophantic, the lie, the totally broken contract, the recreation, the assertion, the favour, and the anihilation, could either form wholes to the left or wholes to the right . . . depending, Father Vea thought, on whether the new changes came from internal or external necessity. 'I am looking for the most rotten man in politics,' asserted the giantman, 'for when I get him, I will purify him, and make him the favourite for the new Jesus Christ.' And the ministers seemed to be dancing a history-hip dance, for the giantman was giving them a deep vindication: he was not coming to destroy the leaders but only those under them. And to manoeuvre in governing was to show ability, and above all to create value: for how else could they be chosen candidates for the biggest post in the skies? Was God not the most tremendous political arranger in the world? All the same, bronzeman pulverised the belly of one minister with short sharp blows, and left him for dead. 'The dead minister was the most rotten least principled man among us,' one minister said with regret: if only he could be the boss of the skies instead! 'Where is your leader?' the aerial visitor with the murderous hands demanded. 'He has gone looking for you at the valleys to strike a deal for the whole country.' Everything has an end, Father Vea caught himself whispering in exhaustion. 'I will add the leader to the dead minister as another two candidates,' stated bronzeman, dragging Vea along with him again. The lorry of wooden gold had already come and taken the dead man to the valleys. What old old eyes the giantman had, as he wiped the blood on his hand. His broad knees could hit any metal freely and survive. 'I am completely neutral to your life and to your death,' he said with a snort into the sky.

One tree received the shade of another and Father Vea and the bronzeman went back towards the town, out of the yellow city with its stunned crowds helpless against the driver of lorrygold. All of Father Vea's African Gonja karate was finished, and he could hardly walk. Neither were his bruised knees allowed to pray. 'But I am also a religious man,' the Greatgold Driver was saying, 'and the only differ- ence between your religion and mine is distance. From the galaxies your worshipping at the shrine and at the altar looks ridiculously small, and you have nothing of real power to look back at us on an equal basis. And it was the unending sympathy of the Lord – do you know that he was at first a warrior of the stars? – that led me to kill him. Too much spirit for a man of power and gadgets!' The giant laughter had come again, but when he laughed his eyes remained neutral, his dark tight skin getting tighter with its glowing.

No one man, no one people will ever control the universe, Father Vea thought, limping in and out of his utter despair. If anyone succeeds in the process of doing so, then we could all see the terrible narrowness of the galaxies, see the desire to murder the spirit. But the spirit will live and make for another corner of the stars. Father Vea stopped, and looked curiously at the giantman. He said to the giant, 'There's no need to convert any of us into a spirit to fill the vacancy of the Lord, for the spirit of the Lord is indivisible . . . and if you rule the universe alone, you will only be trapped in your own inventions. We are not afraid of exclusive and powerful people of the skies, and as we raise the level of the spirit, you will find us dangerous to your narrow world, and impossible to destroy!'

Bishop Bawa was standing waiting for giantman and Father Vea at the outskirts of the town, among the neem leaves and the snake-plants.

He was with the little girl of shades, and the shrine herbalist. Giantman stopped in anger. 'We have come with a new spirit to defeat you, to show you that no matter how powerful you are, we know your secret: spirit for us and spirit for a man of the galaxies is the same, is indivisible.' The giant took his look of intense concentration, for he could not see nor make radio contact with the wooden gold lorry. He marched forward with his huge strides to slap Father Vea, but Vea had crawled swiftly to the side of the small party with the bishop at the head of it.

'You can't kill anyone again in this town! Your power to kill is finished for a year because you have overused it . . .' shouted the little girl, with her head in her hands and herbs on her neck. And Father Vea shouted, 'The biggest secret that you have and you don't want to tell us is that the flesh is not the home of the spirit! Spirit is the indivisible atom, the atom's atom's atom!' The herbal man was outstaring the bronzeman, and holding roots together. The giant's face looked more and more intense, and he looked as if he were rooted to the spot. 'And owura Giant,' screamed the little girl, 'look up at the sky! Don't you see your lorry of wooden gold being pulled up the sky? It is climbing its own rope without you!' 'Yes!' added Bishop Bawa. 'You came to us as the master of the skies and so, dear master, where is your mastery now!' 'But we haven't defeated him yet, we haven't defeated him yet. He is trying to ask for extra energy from his originators! But the originators hate energy asked for in advance! So we will not dance too soon!' shouted the herbal man.

'Give him images and strange but true stories! Fill his mind with our world, for that is the only way of defeating his concentration.' The bishop was running about with hands held high. Father Vea shouted as the lorry of wooden gold continued to rise into the skies, 'We know your secret experiments that speak about spiritual vacancies, the lizard burst before its own white eggs, we have layers of air that carry a lorry that obeys its originators for the right reasons but wrong in the eyes of the masters, we have never seen in the galaxies the honeysuckle under the heel of wild wired men from other planets, the sense of irrepressible birds forming one line and one wing all the way to the real master of the universe who does not boast of his mastery, and all we needed was a child of the tropics with insights that travel through evil, VACANCY FOR THE POST OF JESUS CHRIST INDEED!'

And the giantman was shrinking, but he shrank only two inches, for his will was only enough for his height; but this will was never enough to keep the lorrygold. 'But where's the historical room?' bronzeman asked, his voice less neutral now, full of the tones of doubt. 'It's an open-air room right here in the presence of the different generations standing before you,' Father Vea answered. 'Will the dead you murdered remain dead?' asked the herbal shrine man. 'Look, look, look up on top of the lorrygold almost gone see something!' the shade girl shouted.

Up there among the few guavas left at the back of the truck stood, still alive, the victims of the anger of the giantman. And they were waving. And who was that dusky bearded man in the white robes, immediately above the lorrygold, the man just jumped down from a sudden cross in the sky, and looking with wonder at the nailmarks on his hands? 'Lord!' shouted Father Vea in a trance. 'I knew you would come from the freest most difficult part of the universe! Only your humility in the helicopter! I knew you would arrive in this proud and clean tropical land . . .' The little girl of shades and spirit asked the disappearing dark Jesus, 'Please, O son of the universal Controller, can you please show us your appointment letter from God?' The cynical raised their eyebrows, the wise nodded, the poor and the rich had one reaction, and the animals were free . . . and the giantman groaned, almost human now. But had he found his peace?

BIOGRAPHICAL NOTES

CHIGBO, OKEY Born in Enugu, Nigeria in 1955, Chigbo attended secondary school in that city. He moved to Canada in 1976, and gained a BA in Economics from Simon Fraser University, Vancouver. His articles have been published in *West Africa*, *New African*, *African Events*, *Class*, *Black Enterprise*, *Canadian Business*, *Toronto Life* and *The Business Journal*. He is a contributing editor for *The Business Journal* in Toronto, and works freelance for *Canadian Business* as a fact checker. His first published short story, 'The Chief Clerk's Choice', recently appeared in *The African Letter*, Toronto.

CHIMOMBO, STEVE Born in Zomba, Malawi, in 1945, Chimombo is currently Professor of English at Chancellor College, University of Malawi. He has written one novel, *The Basket Girl*, a collection of short stories, *Tell Me a Story*, and a book on Malawian oral literature, plays and short stories. In 1976 he won first prize in the British Council National Short Story Writing Competition. He is also well known as a poet whose volume, *Napola Poems* (Zomba: Manchici Publishers, 1987), received honourable mention in the 1988 Noma Award.

COUTO, MIA Born in Beira, Mozambique, in 1955, Couto has been director of the Mozambique Information Agency (AIM), the magazine *Tempo* and the daily newspaper *Noticias*. His first volume of poetry, *Raíz de orvalho* (Root of Dew), was published in 1983. His collection of stories, *Voces anoitecidas*, published in 1986 in Mozambique, was subsequently published in Portugal and Italy. Some of the stories have been adapted for radio and stage. David Brookshaw's English translation of the stories has been published by Heinemann International (1990) as *Voices Made Night*.

DJEBAR, ASSIA Born in Cherchel, Algeria, in 1936, Djebar is known as the major woman writer from the Magreb. Her first novel, *La Soif* (Paris: Juillard), was published in 1957. Since then she has published several novels, a play, short stories and articles, a number of which have been translated into English. She also writes in Arabic and her film, *La Nouba des femmes du Mont Chenoua*, was awarded the Critics' Prize at the Venice Biennale in 1979. She is also a historian who has taught at the University of Algiers since 1962.

DONGALA, E. B. A poet, novelist and short-story writer from the Congo, Dongala has been described as one of Africa's leading satirists. Born in 1941, he went to school in the Congo before studying science in the United States and France and teaching chemistry at the Universities of Strasbourg and Brazzaville. He has published one novel, *Un fusil dans la main, un poème dans la poche* (Paris: Albin Michel, 1973), and a collection of stories, *Jazz et vin de palme* (Paris: Hatier, 1982), which has been banned in the Congo. 'The Man' is taken from this collection.

GORDIMER, NADINE Born in 1923, Gordimer is one of South Africa's best-known writers. She has published more than twenty books, including essays, short-story collections and novels. Her novel, *The Conservationist* (London: Jonathan Cape, 1974), was awarded the Booker Prize (UK) in 1974 and also the French International Literary Prize, Le Grand Aigle d'Or, in 1975. Her most recently published novel is *My Son's Story* (London: Bloomsbury, 1990). She won the Nobel Prize for Literature in 1991.

GURNAH, ABDULRAZAK Born in Zanzibar in 1948, Gurnah has published three novels, *Memory of Departure* (1987), *Pilgrim's Way* (1988) and *Dottie* (1990). All three are published by Jonathan Cape, London. He now teaches literature at the University of Kent at Canterbury, England, and is working on his fourth novel.

HERZI, SAIDA HAGI-DIRIE A Somali national, was born in Magodishu. She has a BA in English Literature from King Abdulaziz University in Jeddah, Saudi Arabia, and a Master's degree in teaching English from American University in Cairo, Egypt. She is married and has four children; two girls and two boys. She is currently teaching English at King Abdulaziz University in Jeddah.

LAING, KOJO Born in Ghana in 1946, Laing was Secretary to the Institute of African Studies at the University of Ghana and now runs a school in Accra. He has published two novels, *Search Sweet Country* (London: Heinemann, 1986) and *Woman of the Aeroplanes* (London: Heinemann, 1988), and a volume of poetry, *Godhorse* (Oxford: Heinemann International, 1989).

MABUZA, LINDIWE Is South African. Mabuza has been ANC representative in Stockholm, Sweden and is now Chief Representative of the ANC mission to the USA in Washington, DC. A poet and short-story writer, Mabuza edited *One Never Knows*, an anthology of stories by black South African women writers in exile (Braamfontein: Skotaville, 1989).

MAHJOUB, JAMAL Was born in London in 1960, and moved with his Sudanese father and English mother to Khartoum, where he went to school. He has published one novel, *Navigation of a Rainmaker* (Oxford: Heinemann International, 1989), and now lives in Denmark.

MAJA-PEARCE, ADEWALE Was born in London in 1953, and grew up in Lagos. He has published a collection of short stories, *Loyalties and Other Stories* (Harlow: Longman, 1987), and a travelogue, *In My Father's Country* (London: Heinemann, 1987). His most recent publications are *How Many Miles to Babylon?* (Heinemann, 1990) and *Who's Afraid of Wole Soyinka?* (Heinnemann, 1991). He edited the Heinemann Book of African Poetry (1990) and is presently African editor of the journal *Index on Censorship*.

MANDISHONA, DANIEL Is a Zimbabwean writer who has written many short stories. He writes about both urban and rural life.

MATIVO, KYALO Born in Kenya of a traditional peasant family, Mativo began writing and publishing short stories in the 1960s. His work has since been published in journals in Africa, Europe and the United States, and one story has been made into a film for German television. He is currently a freelance writer, actor and film-maker in California.

MOLLEL, TOLOLWA MARTI Is a teacher of drama at the University of Alberta, Edmonton, Canada. Born in Tanzania, his stories have been broadcast on the BBC and published in the *Greenfield Review*, *Kurapipi* and *Okike*.

MUTIA, BA'BILA Born in Victoria (now Limbe), Cameroon, he now teaches African and Modern British Literature at the Ecole Normale Superieure, University of Yaounde. His work has been broadcast on the BBC, and he himself dramatised his Cameroonian *Fireside Tales* in Canadian schools and communities in 1987.

NDEBELE, NJABULO S. Grew up in Western Native Township in Johannesburg and later in Charterston Location, Nigel. He holds an MA from Cambridge and a PhD from Denver University. His collection of stories, *Fools and Other Stories* (Longman) received the Noma Award for publishing in Africa in 1983. Until 1990 Ndebele was the pro vice-chancellor at the National University of Lesotho, where he lived and taught from 1975. In February 1991 he became Professor of African Literature at the University of Witwatersrand.

OKRI, BEN Was born in Nigeria and now lives in London. He has published three novels, *Flowers and Shadows* (Harlow: Longman, 1980), *The Landscapes Within* (Harlow: Longman, 1981) and *The Famished Road* (London: Cape, 1991); also two volumes of short stories, *Incidents at the Shrine* (London: Heinemann, 1986) and *Stars of the New Curfew* (London: Penguin, 1989). In 1987 he was awarded the Commonwealth Writers' Prize for Africa and the *Paris Review* Aga Khan prize for Fiction. *The Famished Road* won the Booker prize in 1991.

SALLAH, TIJAN M. Has published two volumes of poetry and a volume of short stories, *Before the New Earth* (Calcutta: Writers' Workshop, 1988). Born in the Gambia in 1958, Sallah has taught economics at a number of universities in the United States and now works for the World Bank. He is currently editing an anthology of poetry by young West African writers.

VASSANJI M. G. Born in Nairobi in 1950 and educated at the Aga Khan School in Dar es Salaam, Tanzania, the Massachusetts Institute of Technology, and the University of Pennsylvania. He currently lives in Toronto. In 1989 he was an International Visiting Writer at the University of Iowa. His first novel, *The Gunny Sack* (Oxford: Heinemann, 1989), won the 1989 Commonwealth Writers' Prize for the best first novel from Africa. His second novel, *No New Land*, appeared in 1991 (Oxford: Heinemann), and a collection of his short stories, *Uhuru Street*, was published by Heinemann African Writers Series in 1991.